DO Drops
Volume 11

DO Drops
Volume 11

Daily Bible Devotional

Dr. Bo Wagner

Word of His Mouth Publishers
Mooresboro, NC

All Scripture quotations are taken from the **King James Version** of the Bible.

ISBN: 978-1-941039-47-2
Printed in the United States of America
©2023 Dr. Bo Wagner

Word of His Mouth Publishers
Mooresboro, NC
www.wordofhismouth.com

Cover art by Chip Nuhrah

Devotion 1

Esther 1:1 *Now it came to pass in the days of Ahasuerus, (this is Ahasuerus which reigned, from India even unto Ethiopia, over an hundred and seven and twenty provinces:)* **2** *That in those days, when the king Ahasuerus sat on the throne of his kingdom, which was in Shushan the palace,*

In 606 BC, over 2,600 years ago, the southern kingdom of Israel, known as Judah, was taken into captivity in Babylon. The northern kingdom, still called by the name Israel, had been taken captive by Assyria years before. Originally, all of the twelve tribes were together as one nation, but there had been an angry spat in the days of Rehoboam, the son of Solomon, the son of David, and the nation had been split in two. Now, both were gone. The ten northern tribes, Israel, are never shown as having a wholesale return to their homeland. A few came back, but for the most part, they have not been a large presence either in Scripture or in history.

But the history of the two southern tribes, Judah, is followed closely through the Scriptures. When you read the book of Daniel, you are reading about Judah and the seventy-year captivity in Babylon, as seen through the eyes of four Hebrew princes. The book of Ezra tells us about some Jews from the captivity who were allowed to go back to Judah eighty years after captivity was ended to rebuild the temple in Jerusalem. Nehemiah tells us about some Jews who were allowed to go and rebuild the walls of Jerusalem ninety-three years after the captivity was over. And then Esther is about God's people who were still living in what used to be Chaldea with its capital city of Babylon but was now known as Persia (modern-day Iran) with its capital city of Shushan. Babylon had fallen to the Medes and the Persians, and the Persian Empire quickly became the most powerful empire then on Earth. Thousands and thousands of Jews still lived there. Some had gone home, most had stayed behind, but the God that loved them was still the same.

Ahasuerus may have been on the throne where they were, but God was still on the throne of this universe.

DO rest assured that no matter what country, time, or circumstance you are in, God is still in control!

Personal Notes:

_____

_____

_____

_____

_____

_____

_____

_____

_____

_____

_____

_____

Devotion 2

Right off the bat, in the book of Esther, we come across a bat. A dark, bloodthirsty creature named Ahasuerus, king of the Persian Empire. And this king, above all else, was a lover... of himself.

Esther 1:3 *In the third year of his reign, he made a feast unto all his princes and his servants; the power of Persia and Media, the nobles and princes of the provinces, being before him:* **4** *When he shewed the riches of his glorious kingdom and the honour of his excellent majesty many days, even an hundred and fourscore days.*

The opening scene of this book shows Ahasuerus (historians know him by the name Xerxes) throwing a 180-day party in honor of himself. He later extended that for another week for a total of 187 days. And it was specifically to show *"the riches of his glorious kingdom and the honor of his excellent majesty."* In other words, think of a guy wearing an "A" jersey, shaking pom-poms, going, "Two, four, six, eight, who do we think's really great? ME! ME! ME ME ME!"

This is Ahasuerus.

Is it any wonder, then, that he casually chucked his bride aside like a disposable cup and later ordered the genocide of a race of people without even asking who they were or what they had done? Nothing makes a person as dangerous and loathsome as self-absorption.

DO practice these life-enhancing and even life-saving words today: "It's not about me!"

Personal Notes:

_____

_____

_____

_____

_____

_____

_____

_____

_____

_____

_____

_____

_____

_____

_____

_____

_____

_____

_____

_____

_____

_____

_____

_____

_____

_____

_____

_____

_____

Devotion 3

After we are informed of the 187-day "pat me on the back because I am so awesome" drunken party thrown by Ahasuerus, the scene shifts away from Mr. Big Head to a rather remarkable and modest woman.

Esther 1:9 *Also Vashti the queen made a feast for the women in the royal house which belonged to king Ahasuerus.*

Esther is obviously named for the woman who became the queen of the Persian Empire. But before there was ever a Queen Esther, there was a Queen Vashti. And this woman was remarkable in her own right. Her name means beautiful. And it was probably not her birth name. When people came to stay in the court of the king, their names were normally changed. Even Esther's name was different from the one she grew up with; she used to be called Hadassah. So, the fact that she was given the name Vashti tells us that she was an extremely attractive woman.

And yet, as we will see in tomorrow's devotion, she refused to parade her beauty before men to arouse their lusts. She could have had all the attention in the world, but what she wanted more was to do right.

There are not many like her in today's world, sadly. Even among those who call themselves Christians, the mere suggestion that a woman should be modest and not dressed in such a way as to arouse the lust of others is nearly always met with a nuclear explosion type of reaction. But if Vashti had been like those modern "entirely liberated and nearly entirely undressed" so-called Christians, do you realize that we would never even have heard her name? She would have lived and died and been forgotten.

DO be modest, ladies; it matters to God, and it matters to any godly men as well!

Personal Notes:

_____

_____

_____

_____

_____

_____

_____

_____

_____

_____

_____

_____

_____

_____

_____

_____

_____

_____

_____

_____

Devotion 4

With a lecherous pig of a husband, 187 days of booze, and one very attractive wife nearby, disaster was a near certainty. And sure enough…

Esther 1:10 *On the seventh day, when the heart of the king was merry with wine, he commanded Mehuman, Biztha, Harbona, Bigtha, and Abagtha, Zethar, and Carcas, the seven chamberlains that served in the presence of Ahasuerus the king,* **11** *To bring Vashti the queen before the king with the crown royal, to shew the people and the princes her beauty: for she was fair to look on.*

In case you do not really grasp the details, here is the situation: drunk husband sends drunk buddies to order his wife to come and put on "a little show" for all of his drunk buddies.

Well, that is not likely to cause any issues, now is it!

Esther 1:12 *But the queen Vashti refused to come at the king's commandment by his chamberlains: therefore was the king very wroth, and his anger burned in him.*

Some years ago, I heard a lady "Bible teacher" on the radio. A female caller told her that her husband wanted her to go to the local adult bookstore and watch porn videos with him. She, as a Christian, felt uncomfortable doing so. Of all things, this Bible teacher told her, "Oh, dear one, obey your husband in all things; maybe God will make him fall asleep so that you can close your eyes."

The theological term for that belief, by the way, is "stupidity."

Only God deserves all the time, unquestioned obedience; DO give Him that, even if it means disobeying others!

Personal Notes:

_____

_____

_____

_____

_____

_____

_____

_____

_____

_____

_____

_____

_____

_____

_____

_____

_____

_____

_____

_____

_____

_____

_____

Devotion 5

Queen Vashti knew that the laws and customs of the Medes and Persians, as well as simple laws of morality, forbade her from obeying her husband's inappropriate demand. So she refused. The drunken, self-absorbed king then turned to his drunken, self-absorbed buddies for good advice on what to do next. I just cannot imagine how something like that is going to turn out, can you?

Esther 1:19 *If it please the king, let there go a royal commandment from him, and let it be written among the laws of the Persians and the Medes, that it be not altered, That Vashti come no more before king Ahasuerus; and let the king give her royal estate unto another that is better than she.* **20** *And when the king's decree which he shall make shall be published throughout all his empire, (for it is great,) all the wives shall give to their husbands honour, both to great and small.*

Allow me to paraphrase, please. "King, you have the hottest wife on the planet. You should divorce her so that all of our wives will treat us better!" It would take a man whose elevator does not go all the way to the top, whose cheese has slid off of his burger, who is a few French fries short of a happy meal, and whose driveway does not go all the way to the road to agree to something so idiotic.

Ahasuerus was all that and more. But what more can you expect from a drunk? His foolishness did not start on this day; it started on the very first day he ever put alcohol to his lips and only went downhill from there.

Not one good thing ever comes from drinking alcohol. Not. One.

DO be smarter than Ahasuerus. DO stay away from booze entirely!

Personal Notes:

_____

_____

_____

_____

_____

_____

_____

_____

_____

_____

_____

_____

_____

_____

_____

_____

_____

_____

_____

_____

_____

_____

_____

_____

_____

Devotion 6

Not only did Ahasuerus divorce his lovely wife in a drunken fit of rage, he also decided to dash off an angry letter… to the entire world.

Esther 1:22 *For he sent letters into all the king's provinces, into every province according to the writing thereof, and to every people after their language, that every man should bear rule in his own house, and that it should be published according to the language of every people.*

Reading the text of this letter, any astute Bible student will immediately recognize a similarity between it and a New Testament passage of Scripture.

Ephesians 5:22 *Wives, submit yourselves unto your own husbands, as unto the Lord.* **23** *For the husband is the head of the wife, even as Christ is the head of the church: and he is the saviour of the body.* **24** *Therefore as the church is subject unto Christ, so let the wives be to their own husbands in every thing.*

If you think those two passages are essentially the same, you are entirely correct. And yet, the first one is flawed, and the second one is unflawed. How, you ask, is it possible for the content to be the same and yet one be flawed while the other unflawed? It is simple, really. A message can be flawed either in the content of the message or the character of the messenger. The husbands who are to bear rule in Ephesians 5 are also told to love their wives as Christ loved the church and gave Himself for it. There is absolutely none of that attitude in the message of Ahasuerus; it is simply, "Men are manly, manly men; women must stay in their place."

The theological term for that belief, by the way, is "horse's rear end."

Men, don't worry about your wife submitting to you. DO love her like Christ loves the church, and that will almost assuredly happen without you even having to try!

Personal Notes:

_____

_____

_____

_____

_____

_____

_____

_____

_____

_____

_____

_____

_____

_____

_____

_____

_____

_____

_____

_____

_____

Devotion 7

The thing about being a drunken idiot is that eventually you sober up and have to face up to the problems you have caused yourself and others. And that was certainly true of Ahasuerus.

Esther 2:1 *After these things, when the wrath of king Ahasuerus was appeased, he remembered Vashti, and what she had done, and what was decreed against her.* **2** *Then said the king's servants that ministered unto him, Let there be fair young virgins sought for the king:* **3** *And let the king appoint officers in all the provinces of his kingdom, that they may gather together all the fair young virgins unto Shushan the palace, to the house of the women, unto the custody of Hege the king's chamberlain, keeper of the women; and let their things for purification be given them:* **4** *And let the maiden which pleaseth the king be queen instead of Vashti. And the thing pleased the king; and he did so.*

Ahasuerus was not drunk anymore. Ahasuerus was not angry anymore. But Ahasuerus was also not married to lovely Vashti anymore, and the laws of the Medes and the Persians made it impossible for him to do anything about that. So now, the drunken buddies who suggested that he divorce her were in a bind; the most hot-tempered man in the world was now "single and needy," and they all still had their wives. That was enough to get them all killed, resuscitated, and killed again, and they knew it. So they came up with the idea of a beauty pageant to find a new wife for the king. It was like an early version of "Persian Bachelor."

It was also what God used to save His people. God took a horrible situation and brought great good out of it. He's pretty good at that.

DO remember that whatever happens in the life of a child of God, even the bad stuff, God will bring good stuff out of it!

Personal Notes:

_____

_____

_____

_____

_____

_____

_____

_____

_____

_____

_____

_____

_____

_____

_____

_____

_____

_____

_____

_____

Devotion 8

When we were first introduced to King Ahasuerus, it was at a 187-day drunken party, a "pat me on the back because I am so awesome" pep rally. But something you should know is that the pep rally was designed to rally the troops for a specific purpose. The king was getting ready to lead his forces into battle against Greece. And that explains a little matter of timing given to us in the book of Esther. According to Esther 1:3, this feast and the disaster that followed took place in the third year of his reign. But look at when Esther became his new queen:

Esther 2:16 *So Esther was taken unto king Ahasuerus into his house royal in the tenth month, which is the month Tebeth, in the seventh year of his reign.*

The king was divorced for four years before Esther became the new queen! We will see the details of her becoming queen over the next few devotions, but for now, I just want you to understand that the war with Greece and the king's eventual return took four years. History bears that biblical fact out. So a king, in a drunken rage, destroys his home, sobers up the next day, realizes what he has done and that he is without his wife, and then has to march off to battle for the next four years. Any guesses on how that went?

In a word, horribawfuterrible. Greece cleaned the clock of Ahasuerus and Persia. Ahasuerus had to slink home like a whipped dog. Did the destruction of the home cause all of this? Probably not. But did the destruction of the home heavily contribute to all of this? Unquestionably. When things are a disaster in the home, it inevitably bleeds over into work and play and worship and every other aspect of life.

DO keep your home in good shape if you expect everything else in your life to stay in good shape!

Personal Notes:

_____
_____
_____
_____
_____
_____
_____
_____
_____
_____
_____
_____
_____
_____
_____
_____
_____
_____
_____
_____

Devotion 9

The advisors to the king had suggested a pageant to choose the new queen. But as we begin to be informed about the pageant itself, a new character is introduced to the narrative, and he is the most unlikely of characters to find in all of this.

Esther 2:5 *Now in Shushan the palace there was a certain Jew, whose name was Mordecai, the son of Jair, the son of Shimei, the son of Kish, a Benjamite;* **6** *Who had been carried away from Jerusalem with the captivity which had been carried away with Jeconiah king of Judah, whom Nebuchadnezzar the king of Babylon had carried away.*

This man, Mordecai, seemingly came out of nowhere to become one of the most important men who has ever lived. But in these few words about him, we find that he actually came from a rather significant "somewhere." We are told that he was the son of Jair, the son of Shimei, the son of Kish, a Benjamite." But as is so often the case with Jewish genealogies, some of these names were the names of men far back in his history, not the names of his father and grandfather and great-grandfather. And while Jair was likely his father and the one taken into captivity in verse six, two of those names trace back to the very first generation of the monarchy in Israel. Shimei was the jerk who, in 2 Samuel 16:5, cursed David and threw rocks at him in one of his worst moments. He did so because he was from the line of the other famous name mentioned here in Esther, a man named Kish.

And Kish was the father of Saul, the first king of Israel. This man, Mordecai, was royalty. Under other circumstances, he could have been the one with the crown on his head. And yet, here we find him quietly serving in the court of the king of Persia. And as the book progresses, we will find him helping to save the people over whom he could have been king.

DO be aware as you go about your day that the "common people" that we humans interact with likely have far more to them than meets the eye... including you!

Personal Notes:

_____
_____
_____
_____
_____
_____
_____
_____
_____
_____
_____
_____
_____
_____
_____
_____
_____
_____

Devotion 10

After introducing us to Mordecai, the text tells us about a family responsibility that he stepped up to the plate and took care of.

Esther 2:7 *And he brought up Hadassah, that is, Esther, his uncle's daughter: for she had neither father nor mother, and the maid was fair and beautiful; whom Mordecai, when her father and mother were dead, took for his own daughter.*

Pop quiz for you. We see that Mordecai took his young cousin Esther into his home and raised her as if she were his own daughter after her parents died. So, how old do you think Mordecai was, this man who took on the responsibility of fatherhood for this precious young lady?

Are you ready for a surprise? Based on the information we find in verse six about the timing of his captivity, he was probably in his mid to late 90s! He was not just old enough to be her father; he was old enough to be her great-grandfather!

I wonder what was going through his mind as he considered whether he could do this or not. Would he have the strength? Would his thoughts still be clear enough to be able to guide a girl into womanhood successfully? You know that he had to wonder whether or not he was up to the task. And yet, fears or no, doubts or no, he simply stepped up and did what needed to be done, and because of that, ended up being the cause of the entire Jewish nation surviving an attempted genocide.

So, you there, the person who wonders whether or not you are up to the task God has given you, just DO it! You never know how big of a difference you may make when you do.

Personal Notes:

_____
_____
_____
_____
_____
_____
_____
_____
_____
_____
_____
_____
_____
_____
_____
_____
_____
_____
_____
_____
_____
_____
_____
_____
_____

Devotion 11

We have learned of Ahasuerus, we have learned of Mordecai, and now Esther, the star of the book, will begin to take center stage.

Esther 2:8 *So it came to pass, when the king's commandment and his decree was heard, and when many maidens were gathered together unto Shushan the palace, to the custody of Hegai, that Esther was brought also unto the king's house, to the custody of Hegai, keeper of the women.* **9** *And the maiden pleased him, and she obtained kindness of him; and he speedily gave her her things for purification, with such things as belonged to her, and seven maidens, which were meet to be given her, out of the king's house: and he preferred her and her maids unto the best place of the house of the women.*

From all over the Persian Empire, the vast majority of the known world, lovely young ladies were gathered for this pageant. And yet, living right there in the palace was this young lady named Hadassah, who would become known as Esther. She was noticed, she was drafted into the pageant, and she quickly became the favorite of a man named Hegai, who was in charge of preparing all of these young women to meet the king. Out of one hundred twenty-seven provinces stretching from India all the way to Ethiopia, the one girl who could potentially save the lives of the entire nation of Israel "just so happened" to already be right there under the king's nose, and "just so happened" to immediately become the favorite of the man who ran the pageant...

As you may have surmised, there is never any such thing as "just so happened" with God. This was not serendipity; it was sovereignty! It was the God who knows everything, putting the chess pieces in the right place on the board before the contest even started. Don't you know the devil has to just hate playing God in chess...

When you get worried about all of the frightening, uncontrollable things happening in the world around you, DO remember that God always has His needed pieces in place before the contest ever begins!

Personal Notes:

_____
_____
_____
_____
_____
_____
_____
_____
_____
_____
_____
_____
_____
_____
_____

Devotion 12

In the midst of all the "hugeness" of things like a royal divorce, a disastrous war, and a beauty pageant to decide the next queen, it was actually something very small comparatively that made the biggest difference in all of the events of the book of Esther.

Esther 2:10 *Esther had not shewed her people nor her kindred: for Mordecai had charged her that she should not shew it.*

That verse is, at once, both sad and instructive. It is sad that Mordecai even had to give Esther this instruction. It is sad that even way back then, anti-Semitism was alive and well. It is sad that it has survived and thrived even into our day. But the instructive part of this verse is that a young woman being raised by an aged cousin as if he were her father still regarded his wisdom as good and his words as law. He told Esther not to tell anyone that she was a Jew, and she obeyed without any pushback. In fact, look at how verse twenty puts it:

Esther 2:20 *Esther had not yet shewed her kindred nor her people; as Mordecai had charged her: for Esther did the commandment of Mordecai, like as when she was brought up with him.*

Esther, as a young adult, still obeyed her adoptive father as quickly and fully as if she were still a child in his house. If young people were in the habit of mimicking that pattern in their lives today, there would be almost no drunkenness or pregnancies out of wedlock or crime across our entire land. Instead, when young people get into their mid or late teens, they often decide that they are wiser than their parents and refuse to listen and obey any longer.

And the disastrous results that almost always follow are entirely predictable.

Young people, DO keep on listening to your parents well on up into your young adult years; they have already walked the path that you are all on and want nothing better than to see you walk it safely and successfully!

Personal Notes:

_____

_____

_____

_____

_____

_____

_____

_____

_____

_____

_____

_____

_____

_____

_____

_____

_____

_____

_____

Devotion 13

There came a day when King Ahasuerus was back from war. He was in a foul mood, nursing his wounds, brooding over his losses, and plotting his revenge. In the meantime, he needed to go ahead and select a new wife.

Esther 2:12 *Now when every maid's turn was come to go in to king Ahasuerus, after that she had been twelve months, according to the manner of the women, (for so were the days of their purifications accomplished, to wit, six months with oil of myrrh, and six months with sweet odours, and with other things for the purifying of the women;)* **13** *Then thus came every maiden unto the king; whatsoever she desired was given her to go with her out of the house of the women unto the king's house.* **14** *In the evening she went, and on the morrow she returned into the second house of the women, to the custody of Shaashgaz, the king's chamberlain, which kept the concubines: she came in unto the king no more, except the king delighted in her, and that she were called by name.*

All of the women had undergone ceremonial purification, and they had also been oiled, perfumed, coiffed, shaped, tanned, toned, trimmed, and gussied up. Then, one by one, they went for a night with the king, each one becoming either a "B-list" wife or the one and only "A-list" wife. From that point on, all of the B-listers would be little more than concubines, there to serve his whims from time to time.

You say, "That is terrible and wicked!" And you are correct. Welcome to how things were done in the godless, pagan, ancient world. But do you know what finally changed it around the world? Christianity. It had already been radically different under Judaism, but only one nation was affected by that. When Christianity swept across the globe, it brought with it radical commands that taught men to be monogamous and loving and faithful and sacrificial toward their wives.

Ladies, DO thank God for the wonderful lives you have been provided through Christianity when compared with the debauchery of the ancient world!

Personal Notes:

_____
_____
_____
_____
_____
_____
_____
_____
_____
_____
_____
_____
_____
_____

Devotion 14

The loveliest ladies in the empire were now being brought in to the king one by one to see which one he would choose as the new queen. Physically, all of them were no doubt utterly stunning; there would be no ugly ducklings in this group, or the person in charge of the pageant would forfeit his life.

But if all of those ladies were so beautiful, how would one manage to rise above another in his sight? Here is your answer.

Esther 2:15 *Now when the turn of Esther, the daughter of Abihail the uncle of Mordecai, who had taken her for his daughter, was come to go in unto the king, she required nothing but what Hegai the king's chamberlain, the keeper of the women, appointed. And Esther obtained favour in the sight of all them that looked upon her.*

In verse thirteen, we learned that each woman going before the king could ask for whatever she wanted as she did so, be it jewelry or elegant clothing or anything she felt was needed for the night. But when Esther's turn came, she simply said to the king's chamberlain, "Whatever you think is best, that's what I'll go with." Little wonder then that Esther *"obtained favor in the sight of all them that looked upon her."* Do you realize that *"all them that looked upon her"* even included her competition? Esther truly did have an amazingly sweet spirit! It set her apart from everyone else, and in verses sixteen and seventeen, we learn that the king chose her as his new queen.

In case you do not know, this should not just be "a girl thing." Every child of God, male or female, should have such a sweet spirit that we stand apart from the typical ungrateful, self-centered crowd this world produces.

DO have such a spirit!

Personal Notes:

_____
_____
_____
_____
_____
_____
_____
_____
_____
_____
_____
_____
_____
_____
_____
_____
_____
_____
_____
_____
_____

Devotion 15

Here is the account of Esther officially becoming the new queen and the king's reaction to it:

Esther 2:16 *So Esther was taken unto king Ahasuerus into his house royal in the tenth month, which is the month Tebeth, in the seventh year of his reign.* **17** *And the king loved Esther above all the women, and she obtained grace and favour in his sight more than all the virgins; so that he set the royal crown upon her head, and made her queen instead of Vashti.*

He set the royal crown upon her head and made her queen...

You are looking at something far more unique than you may realize. In a previous devotion, we looked at the background of Mordecai. We found that he was descended from the family of Kish, the father of Saul, the first king of Israel. He was royalty, and no one knew it. But that means that Esther, his cousin, was also royalty without anyone knowing it.

The empire of Ahasuerus was 4,000 miles from tip to tip and had around one hundred million people in it. A beauty pageant is staged, and they bring in hundreds of girls from across the known world. Yet out of an empire 4,000 miles long, nearly two and a half million square miles of landmass, with one hundred million people, there is a girl right there in the palace under his nose, a girl that God regards as being descended from royalty, ready to be the next queen of Persia. And she "just so happens" to be chosen out of all the rest!

DO be continually amazed at how great our God is. Even when you cannot see His hand, His hand is in control!

Personal Notes:

_____

_____

_____

_____

_____

_____

_____

_____

_____

_____

_____

_____

_____

_____

_____

_____

_____

_____

_____

_____

_____

_____

_____

_____

_____

Devotion 16

The book of Esther is a true, historical drama that is so filled with intrigue and adventure that no Hollywood writer could even top it even utilizing pure fiction. After we are informed that Esther has become the new queen, we are then made aware of a "behind-the-scenes" aspect of the drama.

Esther 2:21 *In those days, while Mordecai sat in the king's gate, two of the king's chamberlains, Bigthan and Teresh, of those which kept the door, were wroth, and sought to lay hand on the king Ahasuerus.* **22** *And the thing was known to Mordecai, who told it unto Esther the queen; and Esther certified the king thereof in Mordecai's name.*

While everyone out in the open was celebrating the new queen, two villains in the shadows were plotting an assassination. And unlike most people in Persia, they were actually in a position to carry it out. They were the king's chamberlains, men who were "threshold watchers," guarders of the king's door. In that position, they almost certainly would have gotten by with what they were plotting, save for one thing. A very old man "just so happened" to overhear their plot, and that very old man "just so happened" to be Mordecai, who "just so happened" to be the adoptive father of the new Queen, Esther.

Needless to say, things did not end very well for those men:

Esther 2:23 *And when inquisition was made of the matter, it was found out; therefore they were both hanged on a tree: and it was written in the book of the chronicles before the king.*

An old man, who could have simply said, "I'll just let all the young people do the serving," instead chose to continue to keep serving as long as he was living, and in so doing, saved the life of the king, which would eventually result in the king saving the life of all of that old man's people.

Are you still breathing? Then DO keep serving!

Personal Notes:

_____

_____

_____

_____

_____

_____

_____

_____

_____

_____

_____

_____

_____

_____

_____

_____

_____

_____

Devotion 17

Chapter two of the book of Esther ended with Mordecai, Esther's adoptive dad, saving the king's life. But as chapter three begins, that act of valor had been forgotten. In fact, it had been forgotten so quickly that Mordecai had not even been rewarded for it in any way!

Believe me, God was behind the forgetfulness of the king. It was going to be essential for that chip to be cashed in later rather than sooner. Especially since an enemy was about to arise...

Esther 3:1 *After these things did king Ahasuerus promote Haman the son of Hammedatha the Agagite, and advanced him, and set his seat above all the princes that were with him. And all the king's servants, that were in the king's gate, bowed, and reverenced Haman: for the king had so commanded concerning him...*

Haman. Just like the name Esther had a meaning, "star," the name Haman had a meaning as well. Are you ready for this? His name means "magnificent." Now, how in the world does a person like that ever end up as a proud, pompous jerk? I just can't imagine! "Look everybody, here comes... MAGNIFICENT!"

But more significant than that is the fact that he was an Agagite. And here is irony at its finest; just like the background of Mordecai took us all the way back to the days of Saul from whom he was descended, the background of Haman goes back to the exact same place and time. Agag was the king of the Amalekites, the people that Saul was supposed to eradicate. Saul failed to do so, and five hundred years later, a descendent of that Agag the Amalekite became second in command of the Persian Empire and very nearly succeeded in wiping all of the Jews, Saul's people, off the face of the earth.

DO obey today if you want your children and grandchildren to be safe tomorrow and even some tomorrow long after you are gone!

Personal Notes:

_____

_____

_____

_____

_____

_____

_____

_____

_____

_____

_____

_____

_____

_____

_____

_____

_____

_____

_____

Devotion 18

The king had commanded everyone to bow in a show of worship before Haman. But one old man was having nothing of it. And it's not surprising to learn who:

Esther 3:2 *And all the king's servants, that were in the king's gate, bowed, and reverenced Haman: for the king had so commanded concerning him. But Mordecai bowed not, nor did him reverence.*

Throughout the entire book of Esther, we find Mordecai to be absolutely consistent at all times. When his young cousin needed an adoptive father, he took her in because it was the right thing to do. When the king was going to be killed, he saved his life because it was the right thing to do. And now that that same king was ordering him to bow before Haman, he disobeyed the king because it was the right thing to do. You see, this was not a simple bow of respect being required. That kind of bow is perfectly permissible under the Mosaic law and in Jewish life. The bow that was being required was the type that the Persian kings frequently received, a species of divine adoration, a face on the ground and mouth in the dirt worshipful bow.

Many years before there were T-shirt companies printing, "We bow only to God," in reference to the NFL kneeling fiasco, there was one old man all by himself who actually would only bow to God. He knew it could cost him his life, but he was willing to do right anyway.

Always, always, always DO what is right. Mordecai did not become famous across the world for being "agreeable"; he became famous across the world for being principled!

Personal Notes:

_____
_____
_____
_____
_____
_____
_____
_____
_____
_____
_____
_____
_____
_____
_____
_____
_____
_____
_____
_____
_____
_____
_____

Devotion 19

Refusing to bow before a man like Haman was going to go over just about as well as it had a couple of generations earlier when three Hebrew boys named Shadrach, Meshach, and Abednego refused to bow to Nebuchadnezzar's idol. It absolutely would not be unnoticed or overlooked. And sure enough...

Esther 3:3 *Then the king's servants, which were in the king's gate, said unto Mordecai, Why transgressest thou the king's commandment?* **4** *Now it came to pass, when they spake daily unto him, and he hearkened not unto them, that they told Haman, to see whether Mordecai's matters would stand: for he had told them that he was a Jew.*

People who noticed that Mordecai would not bow naturally asked him why. In fact, they did so day after day. But it is the answer that Mordecai gave them that is so very instructive. He did not go into a long lecture or give a sermon or even quote a ton of verses. The only reason he gave them for not bowing was that he was a Jew.

Would there have been anything wrong with a long lecture or a sermon or quoting a ton of verses? Absolutely not. But just by him saying, "I am a Jew," everyone knew all of the things that he would have lectured about, preached a sermon on, or quoted verses concerning!

It ought to be the exact same way with us today. When anyone asks us about things that the

Bible forbids, like drinking or premarital sex or cursing or adultery or homosexuality or lying or stealing or pornography or anything the Bible says is wrong, all we should have to say is, "I'm a Christian," and that should answer all of their questions! But that will only happen if Christians all over the place actually start living the way the Bible teaches on a consistent basis. As long as "Christian" is nothing more than a cool slogan rather than a biblical lifestyle, it will never have the power that it should when we say it.

DO actually behave as a Christian!

Personal Notes:

_____
_____
_____
_____
_____
_____
_____
_____
_____
_____
_____
_____
_____
_____
_____
_____
_____
_____

Devotion 20

One old man refused to bow before one pompous jerk. Unfortunately, the one pompous jerk was not willing to let this be just an issue between him and the one old man.

Esther 3:5 *And when Haman saw that Mordecai bowed not, nor did him reverence, then was Haman full of wrath.* **6** *And he thought scorn to lay hands on Mordecai alone; for they had shewed him the people of Mordecai: wherefore Haman sought to destroy all the Jews that were throughout the whole kingdom of Ahasuerus, even the people of Mordecai.*

Haman knew who he himself was and what people he was descended from. Now, he also knew who Mordecai was and what people Mordecai was descended from. He knew from history that his people had tried to destroy the Jews and that the Jews had, in turn, tried to destroy them. It didn't work in either case. But now things were different. Now, Amalek and Israel were not on even footing. Now, Amalek had a descendent of Agag second in command of the most powerful nation on earth, and the Jews were just powerless subjects without an army. This was Haman's chance to finish the job that his forefathers had started and get personal vengeance on Mordecai as well.

Isn't it interesting how many times both in Scripture and in our everyday lives, we experience a negative "blast from the past?" And isn't it also interesting how very many times all of those "blasts" could have been avoided if we had simply done right "way back there!"

We cannot change the PAST, but we can change the FUTURE by doing right in the PRESENT. So DO so!

Personal Notes:

_____
_____
_____
_____
_____
_____
_____
_____
_____
_____
_____
_____
_____
_____
_____
_____
_____
_____
_____
_____
_____
_____
_____
_____
_____
_____

Devotion 21

Haman was determined to eradicate the Jews. But, being the typical superstitious Middle Easterner of that day, he wanted to make sure that he got "fate" on his side by picking just the right day for the endeavor.

Esther 3:7 *In the first month, that is, the month Nisan, in the twelfth year of king Ahasuerus, they cast Pur, that is, the lot, before Haman from day to day, and from month to month, to the twelfth month, that is, the month Adar.*

Esther and the king had been married for four or five years now. Sometime during those five years, Mordecai had saved the king's life, and it had been forgotten. Now, Haman is going to try to kill Mordecai and all his people. And by the use of "Pur," which was something like dice, they determined that the best time to do this was the middle of the month Adar.

They rolled the dice on the first month of the year; it told them to destroy the Jews on the very last month of the year.

Let that sink in…

If the Pur had told them to do the genocide the very next month, what would be the odds of them finding out about it and being able to prepare themselves to survive it? Zero, absolutely zero. But somehow, it "just so happened" (isn't it amazing how many times we see that concerning the book of

Esther?) that they ended up with the maximum amount of time possible to prepare for this!

The God who controls the tides of the day also controls the tumble of the dice.

DO have confidence that even in the terrifying things, God is still in control!

Personal Notes:

_____
_____
_____
_____
_____
_____
_____
_____
_____
_____
_____
_____
_____
_____
_____
_____
_____
_____
_____
_____
_____
_____
_____
_____
_____

Devotion 22

Haman had his plan in place, and he had the day picked out. Now, all he had to do was find a way to get the king to go along with it. And the methodology he adopted was ingenious both in its focus and in its fuzziness.

Esther 3:8 *And Haman said unto king Ahasuerus, There is a certain people scattered abroad and dispersed among the people in all the provinces of thy kingdom; and their laws are diverse from all people; neither keep they the king's laws: therefore it is not for the king's profit to suffer them.* **9** *If it please the king, let it be written that they may be destroyed: and I will pay ten thousand talents of silver to the hands of those that have the charge of the business, to bring it into the king's treasuries.*

There were some things in Haman's sales pitch to the king that (although he was lying) were very specific, very "focused," namely that the king was losing money and that Haman wanted to destroy the people who were costing the king.

But did you notice what he chose to be very vague and "fuzzy" about? Look at the verses again and see if you can figure out what really important detail isn't there:

Esther 3:8 *And Haman said unto king Ahasuerus, There is a certain people scattered abroad and dispersed among the people in all the provinces of thy kingdom; and their laws are diverse* *from all people; neither keep they the king's laws: therefore it is not for the king's profit to suffer them.* **9** *If it please the king, let it be written that they may be destroyed: and I will pay ten thousand talents of silver to the hands of those that have the charge of the business, to bring it into the king's treasuries.*

Do you have it yet? If not, let me help you. The word "Jews" does not appear. He simply used the term "certain people" and then the words their, they, and them. He knew that if he specified the people, that the king would investigate to see if he was telling the truth. And through this, we know that he wasn't telling the truth, meaning that the Jews were model citizens!

DO live your life so above reproach that if anyone wants to lie about you, they cannot do it by using your actual name!

Personal Notes:

_____
_____
_____
_____
_____
_____
_____
_____
_____
_____
_____
_____

Devotion 23

Haman had told his lie to the king, but now he was going to put the cherry on top that he believed was guaranteed to get him what he wanted.

Esther 3:9 *If it please the king, let it be written that they may be destroyed: and I will pay ten thousand talents of silver to the hands of those that have the charge of the business, to bring it into the king's treasuries.*

Killing that many people takes money. And it would also result in a loss of a great deal of tax revenue for the king. These people who were supposedly so awful were actually taxpaying members of society. In one verse, he told the king it was "not for his profit" to let them live, and in the very next verse, he acknowledged that it was going to cost the king a ton to get rid of them.

But to make that palatable to the king, he came and offered to pay for it himself, all of the expenses and losses. And he did so to the tune of 10,000 talents of silver. In today's money, that would be roughly $360 million!

So, is it any real wonder why he became the king's right-hand man? Haman was loaded. And because of that, the king brought that snake up into his bosom.

If you have more than three functioning brain cells, you will be way more careful than that. DO choose your advisors from those who are loyal more than from those who are loaded and those who are straightforward rather than sneaky!

Personal Notes:

_____

_____

_____

_____

_____

_____

_____

_____

_____

_____

_____

_____

_____

_____

_____

_____

_____

_____

_____

_____

_____

_____

_____

_____

_____

Devotion 24

Haman was so bitterly hateful against Mordecai and the Jews that he had offered to pay the sum of $360 million out of his own pocket to see them destroyed. What happened next must have completely blown him away.

Esther 3:10 *And the king took his ring from his hand, and gave it unto Haman the son of Hammedatha the Agagite, the Jews' enemy.* **11** *And the king said unto Haman, The silver is given to thee, the people also, to do with them as it seemeth good to thee.*

Haman was either one of the luckiest men alive or one of the shrewdest men alive, at least up to this point. He offered to pay the king's treasuries all that money to destroy the Jews, and the king basically said, "No, don't worry about that; I'll foot the bill for everything." And then to top that, he gave Haman his signet ring, which, when placed in a blob of wax on a piece of paper, became a seal that made a document unbreakable law. The king basically just handed Haman his own authority. Haman could now write whatever law he wanted and "put the king's signature on it."

There are some things in life that are too valuable to give away, and your good name is one of them.

DO guard your name!

Personal Notes:

_____

_____

_____

_____

_____

_____

_____

_____

_____

_____

_____

_____

_____

_____

_____

_____

_____

_____

_____

_____

_____

_____

_____

_____

Devotion 25

Once Haman had the king's approval and the king's ring, he wasted no time in writing out the very detailed law to destroy the Jews and on what date it was to be done. Those posts were then translated and sent out into all of the languages in all of the king's provinces from India to Ethiopia. They were even posted right there in Shushan the palace where Esther and Mordecai lived.

But it is the reaction the text shows us after this that is so mind-boggling.

Esther 3:15 *The posts went out, being hastened by the king's commandment, and the decree was given in Shushan the palace. And the king and Haman sat down to drink; but the city Shushan was perplexed.*

Reading that "the city Shushan was perplexed" is very understandable. All of them knew that the Jews were model citizens. But the reaction of the king and Haman is not understandable at all. They have just casually signed the death warrant for hundreds of thousands, perhaps even millions of people, and now they are just sitting down to have a drink.

As you might remember, it was that "drinking thing" that started all of the problems in the book of Esther to begin with. To say that Ahasuerus was a slow learner would be far too kind of an evaluation.

Alcohol is evil and destructive and stupefying. DO keep any of it from ever crossing your lips!

Personal Notes:

_____
_____
_____
_____
_____
_____
_____
_____
_____
_____
_____
_____
_____
_____
_____
_____
_____
_____
_____
_____
_____
_____
_____
_____
_____
_____
_____
_____
_____

Devotion 26

Everyone was pretty quickly finding out that a disaster was in the making, including the very man around whom the disaster centered just because he had the audacity to do right.

Esther 4:1 *When Mordecai perceived all that was done, Mordecai rent his clothes, and put on sackcloth with ashes, and went out into the midst of the city, and cried with a loud and a bitter cry;* **2** *And came even before the king's gate: for none might enter into the king's gate clothed with sackcloth.*

Sackcloth was the coarse, rough fabric used to make sacks for carrying produce and other supplies. It would just about peel your skin off, it was so rough. For people to wear it as clothing showed extreme anguish and sorrow.

At other times, to show sorrow, people would put ashes on their heads.

But eight times in the Bible, an unusual thing happened. Eight times, sackcloth and ashes are mentioned together. But in one particular chapter of the Bible, only one, sackcloth and ashes are mentioned twice. That chapter of the Bible is the very one we are now working through. Verse one and verse three show us them using sackcloth and ashes together. Esther 4 marks one of the darkest, most anguish-filled days this world has ever seen.

And because Mordecai had on sackcloth and ashes, he was not allowed to come before the gate of the king. In his hour of greatest need, the king would not see him because the throne always had to be "a happy place."

How much better is our King, King Jesus! Our King says, "Come unto me all ye that labor and are heavy laden…"

DO come before your King, whether it is a silk day or a sackcloth day; He is always glad to see you on either!

Personal Notes:

_____

_____

_____

_____

_____

_____

_____

_____

_____

_____

_____

_____

_____

_____

_____

_____

_____

_____

_____

Devotion 27

It did not take long for Queen Esther to be given the news that her beloved Mordecai was, for some reason, wearing sackcloth and ashes. And as dearly as she loved him, it also did not take her long to try and fix things. But the very fix she provided showed a complete lack of understanding and totally missed the point.

Esther 4:4 *So Esther's maids and her chamberlains came and told it her. Then was the queen exceedingly grieved; and she sent raiment to clothe Mordecai, and to take away his sackcloth from him: but he received it not.*

Do you see the problem? Mordecai was wearing clothing specifically designed to show great anguish of heart. So Esther sent him wonderful new clothes...

Naturally, *"he received it not."* The clothes were not the problem; he doubtless had plenty of clothes, nice, fancy, comfortable clothes. He was wearing what he was wearing because something horrible had happened. He had a huge problem, and Esther, though she meant well, was offering something far less than a solution. She was offering to help a person with a problem look as if they did not have a problem.

We meet people each and every day, and a lot of times, those people have problems. And there is something in us that often gets very uncomfortable when dealing with the problems of others. But if we are going to be like Christ, we are going to have to do more than just help people look like they do not have problems; we are going to have to actually find out what the problem is and how God would like to use us to help them deal with it!

DO be a help to those in trouble, not just a decorator of those in trouble!

Personal Notes:

_____

_____

_____

_____

_____

_____

_____

_____

_____

_____

_____

_____

_____

_____

_____

_____

_____

_____

_____

_____

_____

_____

Devotion 28

When Mordecai refused the clothes that Esther sent to him, she then wisely realized that she should be figuring out what was actually wrong. So she sent a messenger to Mordecai to investigate. And here is how that went.

Esther 4:6 *So Hatach went forth to Mordecai unto the street of the city, which was before the king's gate. 7 And Mordecai told him of all that had happened unto him, and of the sum of the money that Haman had promised to pay to the king's treasuries for the Jews, to destroy them. 8 Also he gave him the copy of the writing of the decree that was given at Shushan to destroy them, to shew it unto Esther, and to declare it unto her, and to charge her that she should go in unto the king, to make supplication unto him, and to make request before him for her people. 9 And Hatach came and told Esther the words of Mordecai.*

There is something instructive in the way that Mordecai handled things. In verse seven, Mordecai TOLD Hatach what was going on. But what he told him was really hard to believe; how could anyone wrap their minds around one man with the desire and the ability to destroy an entire race of people, especially a man respected and trusted by most everyone?

So Mordecai did more than just tell; in verse eight he actually handed him the proof, a copy of the decree.

That is both an effective and fair way to do things. In a world of gossips and cowardly anonymous internet trolls, DO refuse to ever settle for anything less than proof, not innuendo or accusation, and DO always provide proof of the hard-to-believe things that you yourself feel like you have to say!

Personal Notes:

_____
_____
_____
_____
_____
_____
_____
_____
_____
_____
_____
_____
_____
_____
_____
_____
_____
_____
_____
_____
_____

Devotion 29

Mordecai had informed Esther of the problem and asked her to go plead with the king on their behalf. Esther, though, sent back a very disappointing response.

Esther 4:10 *Again Esther spake unto Hatach, and gave him commandment unto Mordecai; 11 All the king's servants, and the people of the king's provinces, do know, that whosoever, whether man or woman, shall come unto the king into the inner court, who is not called, there is one law of his to put him to death, except such to whom the king shall hold out the golden sceptre, that he may live: but I have not been called to come in unto the king these thirty days. 12 And they told to Mordecai Esther's words.*

The king, Esther's husband, had a law; no one was to come into his presence without being called for. In other words, Esther was being asked to (*gasp!*) disobey her husband... just like Vashti before her. And when I point that out, a lot of ladies who have been brainwashed into thinking that Vashti was a disobedient witch and Esther was an angelic heroine are going to pitch a hissy fit, as are the men who have done the brainwashing.

Hiss on; it won't change the fact that you are wrong.

If women are always to obey their husbands at all times no matter what, then both of those ladies were wrong. But the truth is that no one but God deserves one hundred percent, unquestioned obedience at all times. And had Esther taken the easy route and simply "obeyed and hoped for the best," the Jewish people would have ceased to exist.

DO be willing to do what is right before God, even if it means doing what is wrong before man!

Personal Notes:

_____
_____
_____
_____
_____
_____
_____
_____
_____
_____
_____
_____
_____
_____
_____
_____
_____
_____
_____
_____
_____
_____
_____
_____

Devotion 30

There are certain phrases of Scripture that so resonate with us that almost everyone knows them even if they do not know where they are or in what context they were spoken. We find one of those phrases in the answer that Mordecai returned to Esther when she sent word to him that she could not go in and see the king.

Esther 4:13 *Then Mordecai commanded to answer Esther, Think not with thyself that thou shalt escape in the king's house, more than all the Jews.* **14** *For if thou altogether holdest thy peace at this time, then shall there enlargement and deliverance arise to the Jews from another place; but thou and thy father's house shall be destroyed: and who knoweth whether thou art come to the kingdom for such a time as this?*

Mordecai first reminded Esther of a very practical truth; she was actually in greater danger in the palace than the average Jew in the province! Haman wanted to destroy all the Jews, but his particular ire was directed at Mordecai and all his family. Once he found out that Esther was related to Mordecai, he would most certainly see that she ended up dead as well. He would blame that pesky law of the Medes and the Persians to try to save his skin before the king, but he would kill Esther.

But it is then that Mordecai said, "And who knoweth whether thou art come to the kingdom for such a time as this?"

For such a time as this. It is kind of hard to escape the fact that we are in another one of those "for such a time as this" in our own day. This world is openly hostile to biblical truth and to those who hold it. And just as Esther had to reveal herself and take a stand, so must we. Too much is riding on it for us to try to remain safe in anonymity.

DO be willing to stand up and be counted in this wicked, dangerous "such a time as this!"

Personal Notes:

_____
_____
_____
_____
_____
_____
_____
_____
_____
_____
_____
_____
_____
_____
_____
_____
_____
_____
_____
_____

Devotion 31

Esther, precious Esther, absorbed and understood the words of Mordecai. And her glorious character is seen in the answer that she sent back to him.

Esther 4:15 *Then Esther bade them return Mordecai this answer,* **16** *Go, gather together all the Jews that are present in Shushan, and fast ye for me, and neither eat nor drink three days, night or day: I also and my maidens will fast likewise; and so will I go in unto the king, which is not according to the law: and if I perish, I perish.*

Esther was about to face the most difficult task of her life and maybe the last task of her life. But she had enough sense not to do so alone. She asked Mordecai and all the Jews to go before God in fasting for three days. She also got all of her maidens to go before God in fasting for three days.

If the entire fate of our family and our nation were hanging in the balance, when would we go in and see the king? Most likely that very minute without any delay whatsoever! But Esther took three days' time to prepare for it by getting with God. We very much underestimate just how important this is. If there is a God in heaven, and there is, then the absolute most important thing we can do in any circumstance is pray. Yes, Esther needed to go speak to the king. But before she spoke to the king, she needed to speak to THE KING.

Unless the blade of disaster is falling that very second, DO, especially in any difficult circumstance, spend quality alone time with God before doing whatever it is you have to do!

Personal Notes:

_____

_____

_____

_____

_____

_____

_____

_____

_____

_____

_____

_____

_____

_____

_____

_____

_____

_____

_____

_____

_____

_____

_____

_____

Devotion 32

Three days of fasting now done, Esther was as ready as she could hope to be. Now all that was left was to put the plan into action that she had been formulating for those three days.

Esther 5:1 *Now it came to pass on the third day, that Esther put on her royal apparel, and stood in the inner court of the king's house, over against the king's house: and the king sat upon his royal throne in the royal house, over against the gate of the house.* **2** *And it was so, when the king saw Esther the queen standing in the court, that she obtained favour in his sight: and the king held out to Esther the golden sceptre that was in his hand. So Esther drew near, and touched the top of the sceptre.* **3** *Then said the king unto her, What wilt thou, queen Esther? and what is thy request? it shall be even given thee to the half of the kingdom.*

Esther had been fasting for three days. But as she stood before the King, her husband, it is very clear that she did not look like it. She put on her royal apparel, and before she even spoke a single word, we read that the King saw her, and she obtained favor in his sight.

In other words, in this life-and-death battle against wicked Haman, he took the vinegar route, and she took the sugar route. Haman was doom, gloom, and death, which won the first battle of the war, but

Esther was beauty and class and grace, which won the final battle and the war itself.

We will always have battles in this life. And sometimes, we must actually take a negative approach as the situation warrants. But many times, we actually have a choice of which approach to take. And when we do, the graceful approach is always better than the grating approach.

DO learn the power of a classy approach to things!

Personal Notes:

_____

_____

_____

_____

_____

_____

_____

_____

_____

_____

_____

_____

_____

_____

_____

_____

_____

_____

_____

_____

Devotion 33

The king had offered Esther up to half of his kingdom. And she could have cashed in on any physical want of her heart right there on the spot. But since she wanted something of a very different sort, she was going to have to be much more of a chess player and move each piece across the board with a ton of subtlety until she could eliminate the piece that was causing her the most problems. And unfortunately for Haman, Esther was very, very good at that game.

Esther 5:4 *And Esther answered, If it seem good unto the king, let the king and Haman come this day unto the banquet that I have prepared for him.*

Esther showed up unannounced, told the king that she had already prepared a banquet for him and Haman, and asked them to come to it. He had offered her whatever she wanted, and her answer was, in so many words, "I just want you to come for dinner, bay-beee, and you can bring your fiend, I mean 'friend' with you."

Esther could not have been a better spider if she actually had eight legs.

Sometimes in this world of social media, AKA "flying sledgehammers," we often lose what I call "the skill of subtlety." Yes, the devil himself was subtle in the worst of ways in Genesis 3, but that does not mean we should not be subtle in the best of ways as in **Proverbs 1:4**, *"To give subtilty to the simple, to the young man knowledge and discretion."*

DO practice godly subtlety when it is needed!

Personal Notes:

_____

_____

_____

_____

_____

_____

_____

_____

_____

_____

_____

_____

_____

_____

_____

_____

_____

_____

_____

_____

_____

_____

_____

_____

Devotion 34

To say that the king took Esther's bait would be an understatement. He swallowed it hook, line, and sinker and did so enthusiastically:

Esther 5:5 *Then the king said, Cause Haman to make haste, that he may do as Esther hath said. So the king and Haman came to the banquet that Esther had prepared.*

So now Esther had the king and Haman all to herself, her husband, and her would-be assassin. What would she do with this opportunity? Not surprisingly, she would continue setting her trap.

Esther 5:6 *And the king said unto Esther at the banquet of wine, What is thy petition? and it shall be granted thee: and what is thy request? even to the half of the kingdom it shall be performed. 7 Then answered Esther, and said, My petition and my request is; 8 If I have found favour in the sight of the king, and if it please the king to grant my petition, and to perform my request, let the king and Haman come to the banquet that I shall prepare for them, and I will do to morrow as the king hath said.*

For a second time, the king offered Esther anything and asked her what she wanted. And for a second time (and you may mentally insert your best Ray Stevens harem lady voice from "Ahab the Arab here), Esther said, "Heeee heeee heeee, oh, heee heee heee, all I want is for you to come back again tomorrow, crazy crazy crazy!"

What was she doing? Why not just spit it out all at once? Because the more mysterious and alluring she can make herself to her husband, the more he will value her when he realizes that he has to choose between her and Haman. And in those days, that kind of a choice did not always go well for the wife of a powerful man with a powerful friend!

This was a battle of the heart, not just a battle about facts and figures.

DO aim for the heart when fighting a battle for the heart!

Personal Notes:

_____

_____

_____

_____

_____

_____

_____

_____

_____

_____

_____

_____

_____

_____

_____

_____

_____

_____

_____

Devotion 35

Haman, second in command of the Persian Empire, was brash, well-connected, powerful, dangerous... and completely oblivious to the fact that a little woman was playing him like a cheap fiddle.

Esther 5:9a *Then went Haman forth that day joyful and with a glad heart...*

Haman was having himself a very good day! But no sooner had he left the king's presence, he ran into a very familiar thorn in his side:

Esther 5:9b *... but when Haman saw Mordecai in the king's gate, that he stood not up, nor moved for him, he was full of indignation against Mordecai.*

The wording in that verse is specific and hilarious. Wherever it was that Haman was walking, Mordecai was in his way and sitting down. And the old man did not stand up or move at all! Haman had to walk around him to get by. He did not grovel or beg or bow. When it came to righteousness, the man simply did not have a reverse gear.

And every last one of us ought to be the exact same way. When righteousness is going to cost us nothing, we ought to be resolute in our righteousness. When righteousness is going to cost us everything, we ought to be resolute in our righteousness.

DO take a stand (or a seat, in this case) for righteousness!

Personal Notes:

_____
_____
_____
_____
_____
_____
_____
_____
_____
_____
_____
_____
_____
_____
_____
_____
_____
_____
_____
_____
_____
_____
_____
_____
_____
_____
_____
_____

Devotion 36

Pop quiz: if you are taking a very long shot at a head trying to "pop it," would it be easier to hit a very small head or a very big head? Obviously, it would be easier to hit a very big head. And the plan of Esther had taken Haman's already gargantuan head and swelled it to even more epic proportions:

Esther 5:10 *Nevertheless Haman refrained himself: and when he came home, he sent and called for his friends, and Zeresh his wife.* **11** *And Haman told them of the glory of his riches, and the multitude of his children, and all the things wherein the king had promoted him, and how he had advanced him above the princes and servants of the king.* **12** *Haman said moreover, Yea, Esther the queen did let no man come in with the king unto the banquet that she had prepared but myself; and to morrow am I invited unto her also with the king.*

Try and wrap your mind around the fact that this guy literally invited his friends over and called his wife in just to have the opportunity to brag about himself to all of them.

Haman had a weakness; his weakness was that he was wildly, madly in love... with himself. This is a man who would take himself to the prom wearing both the boutonniere and the corsage and demanding to be coronated as both the King and the Queen, and would passionately kiss his lower lip with his upper lip.

People who are stuck on themselves are also stuck with themselves and end up stuck because of themselves.

DO be smart enough not to be stuck on yourself!

Personal Notes:

_____

_____

_____

_____

_____

_____

_____

_____

_____

_____

_____

_____

_____

_____

_____

_____

_____

_____

_____

_____

_____

_____

_____

_____

Devotion 37

We learned in the last devotion that Haman had a fatal weakness, that of being wildly in love with himself. But he also had another weakness that corresponds to that one, one that ultimately rendered him his own executioner. He had just gotten done bragging about how golden his life was, and yet the very next words out of his mouth were these:

Esther 5:13 *Yet all this availeth me nothing, so long as I see Mordecai the Jew sitting at the king's gate.*

All of this availeth me nothing? Do you realize what he was saying? Among other things, he had just gotten done bragging about all of his children. Now he was literally saying that his children meant absolutely nothing to him as long as he had to put up with Mordecai. Gee, thanks, Dad...

The flaw that he was demonstrating here is ungratefulness. He was being handed the world on a silver platter and yet could not enjoy all the blessings that he had unless he could have absolutely positively every single thing he ever wanted. Just like Eve in the garden, all of the countless fruit trees seemed to lose their savor in light of the fact that one tree out of all the garden had fruit that was off-limits.

If you want to be happy about what you have, DO refuse to be unhappy about what you cannot have!

Personal Notes:

Devotion 38

Haman had finished his bragging (about his greatness) and moaning (about Mordecai) session. He had invited everyone over for a praise party, then seamlessly segued into a pity party. It would have been awesome for everyone involved if, at that point, someone, anyone, had possessed the character to say something intelligent like, "Stop whining, you big baby."

Sadly, that kind of advice was not forthcoming from anyone.

Esther 5:14 *Then said Zeresh his wife and all his friends unto him, Let a gallows be made of fifty cubits high, and to morrow speak thou unto the king that Mordecai may be hanged thereon: then go thou in merrily with the king unto the banquet. And the thing pleased Haman; and he caused the gallows to be made.*

Haman had already signed, sealed, and circulated Mordecai's death warrant. All he had to do was bite his tongue until the end of that year, and he could have personally killed the old man on the day of Purim. But instead of reminding him of that, his wife suggested that he make a seventy-five-foot-tall gallows and have Mordecai hung on it.

Sweet chick, that one. (Sarcasm)

Zeresh was apparently as big-headed as Haman. You can tell that by the dimensions of her suggestion. The average Jewish man of those days stood about five foot three inches. A gallows of seven or eight feet would have done the job nicely and been much easier to build. But by hanging him seventy-five feet in the air, everyone would get the message that Haman was not to be trifled with.

Her arrogance and his pride got Haman both killed and humiliated. Funny how that works.

Learn some lessons from the fall of a proud and arrogant family. DO be patient and humble, otherwise, you will, at some point, be the cause of your own embarrassment and ruin!

Personal Notes:

_____

_____

_____

_____

_____

_____

_____

_____

_____

_____

_____

_____

_____

_____

_____

_____

_____

_____

Devotion 39

In a stage drama, the lights will fade on one scene and then rise on another in a different place. And that is very much what happened at this point in the book of Esther. Haman and his cackling bride and their bobble-headed, sycophantic friends had just decided on a seventy-five-foot-tall gallows on which to hang Mordecai. Of course, Haman would need to speak to the king about that first. And so the light goes down on that scene and comes up on another portion of the divine stage, no less a place than the king's own bedchamber...

Esther 6:1a *On that night could not the king sleep...*

Can you see Ahasuerus tossing, turning, clutching the pillow one way, then another? Try as he might, on THAT night, the exact night that Jaffar, I mean, "Haman," was going to come and speak to him about killing Mordecai, the king got a sudden case of insomnia.

And what could a man do about that in the days long, long before Nyquil? Here is your answer:

Esther 6:1b *...and he commanded to bring the book of records of the chronicles; and they were read before the king.* **2** *And it was found written, that Mordecai had told of Bigthana and Teresh, two of the king's chamberlains, the keepers of the door, who sought to lay hand on the king Ahasuerus.*

What are the odds? What are the odds that he would choose having someone read to him as a way to help him sleep, what are the odds that he would choose that exact book out of all possible others, what are the odds that the reader would light on that exact portion out of all of it, and what are the odds all of that would happen on that exact night when it was most needed?

There aren't enough atoms in the universe to write out a number that big.

But there is a God big enough to make the king overlook honoring Mordecai when he should have, give the king insomnia, have him think of that book, and direct the reader to that exact page at that exact perfect moment.

DO hold your arms out as wide as you possibly can... imagine them as being wrapped around the entire universe... and then say, "My God is that big and bigger!"

Personal Notes:

_____
_____
_____
_____
_____
_____
_____
_____
_____
_____

Devotion 40

The king whose sleep had been divinely withheld from him had now been reminded of the time when Mordecai saved his life. And that led to an obvious question for him to ask:

Esther 6:3 *And the king said, What honour and dignity hath been done to Mordecai for this? Then said the king's servants that ministered unto him, There is nothing done for him.*

The records were very clear; Mordecai had saved the king's life, and yet, the king had not so much as thanked him. For an oriental monarch, that was among the most horrifying of failures. But while he was just now realizing this, Mordecai had no doubt had it come to mind very many times over the past few years. Being human, just like all of us, he probably wondered if it had even been worth it to do right, especially now that the very king whose life he saved had signed his death warrant and the death warrant of all his people.

Have you ever been there? Have you ever done something good and kind for another, perhaps even putting yourself at great risk for incurring great loss to do so, only to have no recognition or reward for it whatsoever? Have you perhaps even been savaged by the people to whom you were so kind and selfless? If you have, you have probably not only questioned them but God as well. Sure, human beings can be like that, but why has God not stepped in? But think of this; when did Mordecai really need to be the center of the king's attention, when everything was well in his life and the life of his people, or when his life and the life of his people were about to be exterminated?

God made the king forget so that He could make him remember just when it was needed most.

DO look at your watch or calendar and say these words, "God knows what I do not know, and therefore His timing is perfect!"

Personal Notes:

_____
_____
_____
_____
_____
_____
_____
_____
_____
_____
_____
_____
_____
_____
_____
_____
_____
_____
_____
_____

Devotion 41

The king now knew he had committed a serious "braux pas"* by not rewarding the man who had saved his life. Now, keep in mind that this was the middle of the night. And that is what makes his next question, and the answer to that question, such a remarkable thing.

Esther 6:4 *And the king said, Who is in the court? Now Haman was come into the outward court of the king's house, to speak unto the king to hang Mordecai on the gallows that he had prepared for him. 5 And the king's servants said unto him, Behold, Haman standeth in the court. And the king said, Let him come in.*

Everybody was supposed to be sleeping. But Haman "just so happened" to not be able to sleep because he wanted to ask the king for permission to hang Mordecai, and the king "just so happened" to not be asleep and was therefore reading about that very same Mordecai saving his life!

As I have said so many times already, isn't it interesting how many things "just so happen" for a child of God!

DO trust God with all of your "just so happens!"

*(Wagnerism – from the French faux pas. Wagner definition: a serious violation of the "bro code.")

Personal Notes:

Devotion 42

The king wanted something. Haman wanted something. Those two wants were about to collide, and Haman was going to get the worst of that train wreck.

Esther 6:6 *So Haman came in. And the king said unto him, What shall be done unto the man whom the king delighteth to honour? Now Haman thought in his heart, To whom would the king delight to do honour more than to myself? 7 And Haman answered the king, For the man whom the king delighteth to honour, 8 Let the royal apparel be brought which the king useth to wear, and the horse that the king rideth upon, and the crown royal which is set upon his head: 9 And let this apparel and horse be delivered to the hand of one of the king's most noble princes, that they may array the man withal whom the king delighteth to honour, and bring him on horseback through the street of the city, and proclaim before him, Thus shall it be done to the man whom the king delighteth to honour. 10 Then the king said to Haman, Make haste, and take the apparel and the horse, as thou hast said, and do even so to Mordecai the Jew, that sitteth at the king's gate: let nothing fail of all that thou hast spoken.*

You no doubt see the obvious; even Haman saw the obvious. Haman was going to have to honor the very man he wanted to murder. And yes, that is the most delicious irony and a well-deserved comeuppance for this jerk.

But you may well have missed the less-than-obvious. Haman missed it, too. The less than obvious is that the king just honored Haman as well. Haman told the king to have one of his "most noble princes" honor Mordecai, and the king immediately tagged Haman himself for the job! Yes, he was honoring Mordecai, but he was also honoring Haman by having Haman honor Mordecai. Haman did not see it that way at all; he was crushed and went home in anguish.

How often are we like that?

Not getting our way is not the same thing as not being honored. DO be humble and perceptive enough to see and appreciate honors done to you even when you do not get what you want!

Personal Notes:

_____
_____
_____
_____
_____
_____
_____
_____
_____
_____
_____
_____
_____

Devotion 43

Haman knew better than to contradict the king, or to let him know why he had come to see him to begin with. All he could do was comply and pretend. And that leads to one of the funniest things in human history.

Esther 6:11 *Then took Haman the apparel and the horse, and arrayed Mordecai, and brought him on horseback through the street of the city, and proclaimed before him, Thus shall it be done unto the man whom the king delighteth to honour.* **12** *And Mordecai came again to the king's gate. But Haman hasted to his house mourning, and having his head covered.*

Let all of the details here sink in. It is morning by now. Mordecai has not missed the seventy-five-foot-tall gallows being built. He doubtless knows exactly who it is for. He looks up and sees Haman marching toward him. He is doubtless thinking, "This is the big one, Elizabeth!" Haman marches up to him... stares into his eyes... and says, "Please put on the king's robe and crown. Please get up on the king's horse." Mordecai does, and Haman begins to lead him through the streets, shouting, "Thus shall it be done to the man whom the king delighteth to honor!"

Can you imagine what is going through the mind of Mordecai at that moment? He has got to be thinking, "Only God can do something this epic and this funny!"

For his part, Haman did not think it was epic or funny. Not even a little bit. He went to his house "mourning" with his head covered. He was literally behaving as if the dearest person in life to him had just died!

That is pathetic. When you are mourning over having to be kind to others who have never done you an ounce of harm, you are a rotten person.

DO live your life in such a way that you do not turn fun moments into funeral moments!

Personal Notes:

_____
_____
_____
_____
_____
_____
_____
_____
_____
_____
_____
_____
_____
_____
_____
_____
_____
_____
_____
_____

Devotion 44

It had been the family and friends of Haman that had goaded him into building the gallows on which to hang Mordecai. And it was now those same family and friends that Haman would flee to seeking refuge, comfort, and maybe some warm milk and a blankie. But he was about to be sorely disappointed in that, too.

Esther 6:13 *And Haman told Zeresh his wife and all his friends every thing that had befallen him. Then said his wise men and Zeresh his wife unto him, If Mordecai be of the seed of the Jews, before whom thou hast begun to fall, thou shalt not prevail against him, but shalt surely fall before him.*

If I could paraphrase, they basically just told Haman, "Dude, it must stink to be you; you are TOAST!"

Thanks, peeps.

Poor Haman. He probably thought life could not get any worse at that moment. And if he thought that, he was about to be proven gloriously wrong:

Esther 6:14 *And while they were yet talking with him, came the king's chamberlains, and hasted to bring Haman unto the banquet that Esther had prepared.*

Haman was supposed to be with the king and Esther. He seems to have forgotten that. But a firm knock on the door and an urgent demand from a chamberlain of the king snapped it back to his memory. He knew he had business to attend to.

What he did not know was that he would never see his wife or children again. And as much as he deserved that, it should still tug at our hearts. It should also make us aware of the fact that at some point, we will see the people we love for the very last time, and we may not even be aware of it.

DO soak in every moment with those you love, and DO let them know that you love them!

Personal Notes:

_____
_____
_____
_____
_____
_____
_____
_____
_____
_____
_____
_____
_____
_____
_____
_____
_____
_____
_____
_____

Devotion 45

Haman was now about to have to pretend everything was okay in front of the king and queen. For his part, the king was clearly in a fantastic mood; Esther was really lighting his fire.

Esther 7:1 *So the king and Haman came to banquet with Esther the queen.* **2** *And the king said again unto Esther on the second day at the banquet of wine, What is thy petition, queen Esther? and it shall be granted thee: and what is thy request? and it shall be performed, even to the half of the kingdom.*

For the third time, the king has offered his bride half of the kingdom. Haman had to be amazed at this; it was way, way out of character for Ahasuerus. But if he was surprised at that, that surprise was going to be nothing compared to his next surprise:

Esther 7:3 *Then Esther the queen answered and said, If I have found favour in thy sight, O king, and if it please the king, let my life be given me at my petition, and my people at my request:* **4** *For we are sold, I and my people, to be destroyed, to be slain, and to perish. But if we had been sold for bondmen and bondwomen, I had held my tongue, although the enemy could not countervail the king's damage.*

She was begging for her life and the life of her people. There is no way at all Haman could misunderstand that. He now knew the one critical thing he had not previously known; Esther, the beloved bride of the most hot-tempered, homicidal king in history, was a Jew.

To quote that great theologian, Scooby Doo, "Ruh Roh!"

When you live your life in an underhanded, backstabbing manner, don't be surprised when you find out that others chose not to tell you everything you needed to know.

DO live your life openly, fairly, and honestly, so that will not have to be an issue!

Personal Notes:

_____
_____
_____
_____
_____
_____
_____
_____
_____
_____
_____
_____
_____
_____
_____
_____
_____
_____
_____
_____

Devotion 46

The explosion that was about to happen was predictable:

Esther 7:5 *Then the king Ahasuerus answered and said unto Esther the queen, Who is he, and where is he, that durst presume in his heart to do so?*

Please allow me to paraphrase that Old English phraseology; "Who is the dirtbag that would do such a thing, and where is he? Lemme at him!!!"

There were two people in the room that knew the who and the where. And one of them was, oh, so very ready to spill the beans:

Esther 7:6 *And Esther said, The adversary and enemy is this wicked Haman. Then Haman was afraid before the king and the queen.*

I love the fact that Esther, sweet Esther, called Haman "this wicked Haman." But can you imagine the response her words would receive today from the "Perpetually Pious and Polished Brethren?"

"Tsk! Such unkind language! That tone is likely to turn people away from Christ..."

Pipe down, Mr. Karen. It is entirely right and appropriate to refer to a genocidal maniac as a wicked person, just like it is entirely right and appropriate to refer to child groomers and molesters, rank heretics, and other devils in the flesh as wicked people. And anyone who can consistently find it in their hearts to criticize the children of God but can never find it in their hearts to criticize the children of Satan is like that because they have chosen the side of Team Satan.

DO know that sometimes it is both right and necessary to call someone wicked!

Personal Notes:

_____

_____

_____

_____

_____

_____

_____

_____

_____

_____

_____

_____

_____

_____

_____

_____

_____

_____

_____

_____

_____

_____

_____

_____

_____

Devotion 47

The jig was now up. Esther had wooed her husband with mystery, completely captured his undivided attention, and then exposed Haman, his most trusted advisor, as a genocidal maniac who intended to murder her and all of her people. Needless to say, the king was both furious and floored:

Esther 7:7 *And the king arising from the banquet of wine in his wrath went into the palace garden: and Haman stood up to make a request for his life to Esther the queen; for he saw that there was evil determined against him by the king.*

The king had stormed out of the room into the palace garden in utter fury. And Haman knew that when Ahasuerus walked back in, he was as good as dead. So he stood up to beg and plead with the queen to spare his life.

Let that sink in.

This man, one of the proudest, most arrogant men who has ever lived, a man who despised Jews and doubtless also (as a typical wicked man of his time) disdained women as well, was now being reduced to begging to a Jewish woman. But like some grade B horror movie, he tripped, and of all places, fell flat on the bed Esther was reclining on!

Esther 7:8 *Then the king returned out of the palace garden into the place of the banquet of wine; and Haman was fallen upon the bed whereon Esther was. Then said the king, Will he force the queen also* *before me in the house? As the word went out of the king's mouth, they covered Haman's face.*

When the king said, "Is he going to rape my queen as well?" the guards put a sack over Haman's head. He was now marked for death with no way out. And the last sight he ever saw was the face of the little woman who beat him like a cheap drum.

DO yourself a favor; never underestimate a woman, especially one who knows and walks with God!

Personal Notes:

_____

_____

_____

_____

_____

_____

_____

_____

_____

_____

_____

_____

_____

_____

_____

_____

_____

_____

_____

_____

_____

Devotion 48

Haman now had a bag of death covering his head. The only question at this point was how he was to be killed. We have heard much from the King and Haman and Mordecai and Esther in this book. But suddenly, a new voice speaks up at just that moment.

Esther 7:9 *And Harbonah, one of the chamberlains, said before the king, Behold also, the gallows fifty cubits high, which Haman had made for Mordecai, who had spoken good for the king, standeth in the house of Haman. Then the king said, Hang him thereon.* **10** *So they hanged Haman on the gallows that he had prepared for Mordecai. Then was the king's wrath pacified.*

Who is this guy, Harbonah? We have seen him once before in the book, only without the H at the end of his name:

Esther 1:10 *On the seventh day, when the heart of the king was merry with wine, he commanded Mehuman, Biztha, Harbona, Bigtha, and Abagtha, Zethar, and Carcas, the seven chamberlains that served in the presence of Ahasuerus the king,* **11** *To bring Vashti the queen before the king with the crown royal, to shew the people and the princes her beauty: for she was fair to look on.*

Harbonah was one of those original seven chamberlains who were sent with a message to Queen Vashti that the king demanded her presence. And it would be very easy to assume that he was a dirtbag based on that. But that assumption would be very unfair, for he was not given a chance to speak his own words or thoughts at that moment. In fact, we are not even told that he spoke at all.

But here, several years later, he sees an opportunity to speak, and he does so. And this simple chamberlain, doubtless a eunuch, a guy just tasked with keeping the king's bedroom clean and pleasant, told the king about the gallows, who built it, who he built it for, and what the man he built for had done for the king.

Talk about making your opportunity count! You may not always be given a chance to speak, but when you are, DO make it count!

Personal Notes:

_____

_____

_____

_____

_____

_____

_____

_____

_____

_____

_____

_____

_____

_____

_____

_____

Devotion 49

The body of Haman was now swinging in the wind, seventy-five feet in the air, hung on the gallows that he had built for Mordecai. Talk about a great example of the law of sowing and reaping! But there was still much business to be attended to based on the evil that Haman had already set in motion.

Esther 8:1 *On that day did the king Ahasuerus give the house of Haman the Jews' enemy unto Esther the queen. And Mordecai came before the king; for Esther had told what he was unto her.* **2** *And the king took off his ring, which he had taken from Haman, and gave it unto Mordecai. And Esther set Mordecai over the house of Haman.*

All secrets were now out in the open. The king now knew that, amazingly, the man who had previously saved his life was also Esther's adoptive father. And, after the king gave Esther the house (meaning the family and all the possessions) of wicked Haman, she turned right around and gave all of it to Mordecai to do with as he would. She had learned by long experience to trust his wisdom and judgment. And Mordecai knew just what to do.

Esther 9:10 *The ten sons of Haman the son of Hammedatha, the enemy of the Jews, slew they; but on the spoil laid they not their hand.*

Does it seem overly harsh that Mordecai had the ten sons of Haman put to death? Only if you have completely forgotten what started all of this mess to begin with! It was Saul's failure to kill all of the Agagites hundreds of years before that led to this near-complete extermination of the Jewish people in Mordecai's day. And Mordecai was too wise to repeat that mistake.

None of us are ever likely to be faced with a situation where we have to exterminate an entire family or kingdom in order to keep from being exterminated ourselves. But all of us our daily faced with situations where we have sins and wrong habits and evil associations in our lives and face the temptation to try to "manage" those things rather than completely doing away with them.

Those things and associations in your life that should not be there? DO eliminate them rather than trying to manage them!

Personal Notes:

_____
_____
_____
_____
_____
_____
_____
_____
_____
_____
_____
_____

Devotion 50

What Haman set in motion was not in the least bit affected by his death. Like most evil, it had the capacity to long outlast its creator. And Esther knew this.

Esther 8:3 *And Esther spake yet again before the king, and fell down at his feet, and besought him with tears to put away the mischief of Haman the Agagite, and his device that he had devised against the Jews.* **4** *Then the king held out the golden sceptre toward Esther. So Esther arose, and stood before the king,* **5** *And said, If it please the king, and if I have found favour in his sight, and the thing seem right before the king, and I be pleasing in his eyes, let it be written to reverse the letters devised by Haman the son of Hammedatha the Agagite, which he wrote to destroy the Jews which are in all the king's provinces:* **6** *For how can I endure to see the evil that shall come unto my people? or how can I endure to see the destruction of my kindred?* **7** *Then the king Ahasuerus said unto Esther the queen and to Mordecai the Jew, Behold, I have given Esther the house of Haman, and him they have hanged upon the gallows, because he laid his hand upon the Jews.* **8** *Write ye also for the Jews, as it liketh you, in the king's name, and seal it with the king's ring: for the writing which is written in the king's name, and sealed with the king's ring, may no man reverse.*

An unbreakable writing caused the problem, and therefore an unbreakable writing would be the solution to the problem. What was written could not be unwritten, but it could be combated. And Ahasuerus, absolutely shockingly, gave his wife his ring so that she could write whatever she wanted and sign and seal it as if he himself had done it.

That is the level of trust that should be present in every marriage relationship. So DO conduct yourself within your marriage in such a way that your spouse can trust you like that!

Personal Notes:

_____
_____
_____
_____
_____
_____
_____
_____
_____
_____
_____
_____
_____
_____
_____
_____
_____
_____
_____

Devotion 51

The writing of Haman could not be undone; on the day of Purim, people all over the world were going to try and exterminate the Jews, and it would be one hundred percent legal. But another writing could be sent that would give the Jews a chance to live. And thanks to Mordecai, it was.

Esther 8:9 *Then were the king's scribes called at that time in the third month, that is, the month Sivan, on the three and twentieth day thereof; and it was written according to all that Mordecai commanded unto the Jews, and to the lieutenants, and the deputies and rulers of the provinces which are from India unto Ethiopia, an hundred twenty and seven provinces, unto every province according to the writing thereof, and unto every people after their language, and to the Jews according to their writing, and according to their language.* **10** *And he wrote in the king Ahasuerus' name, and sealed it with the king's ring, and sent letters by posts on horseback, and riders on mules, camels, and young dromedaries:* **11** *Wherein the king granted the Jews which were in every city to gather themselves together, and to stand for their life, to destroy, to slay, and to cause to perish, all the power of the people and province that would assault them, both little ones and women, and to take the spoil of them for a prey,* **12** *Upon one day in all the provinces of king Ahasuerus, namely, upon the thirteenth day of the twelfth month, which is the* *month Adar.* **13** *The copy of the writing for a commandment to be given in every province was published unto all people, and that the Jews should be ready against that day to avenge themselves on their enemies.*

DO hold to two truths from this. One, something can be legal and yet not be right. The holocaust was legal in Germany. Forced slavery was once legal around the world, as is/was abortion. None of them have ever been right. Two, one thing that is right is self-defense! Contrary to the great zeros of the faith, you do not simply have to allow yourself or anyone you love to be assaulted or killed just because you are a believer. Mordecai was a believer and also a very dangerous man, and he made his people very dangerous. And girls, if you are ever involved with a guy who will not fight when needed, please understand that he is not a BAD man; he just isn't a man at all.

Personal Notes:

_____
_____
_____
_____
_____
_____
_____
_____
_____
_____

Devotion 52

There was now a "You Jews can defend yourselves" edict that was going to be sent all across the world. But the "Everybody can kill the Jews" edict already had a sizeable head start! And doubtless, the very finest and fastest posts were used in that first decree, since it was Haman pulling the strings. **Esther 3:15** says, *"The posts went out, being hastened by the king's commandment."* So we have the best animals, the best riders, and the fury of the king making them go at top speed.

But now, we find the pursuers going after that first group:

Esther 8:14 *So the posts that rode upon mules and camels went out, being hastened and pressed on by the king's commandment. And the decree was given at Shushan the palace.*

So, picture all of this, please.

Scene one: "By decree of Ahasuerus, you posts better go at top speed into every province around the world, and don't you dare let anyone or anything catch up to you!

Scene two: "By decree of Ahasuerus, you posts better catch up to those other posts; don't you dare let them beat you to the destination!"

No pressure.

But you see, none of this haste should have even been necessary. All Ahasuerus ever had to do to avoid this massive race across the face of the earth was to sllllooooowwww doooowwwwwnnnn and ask questions first. Just like us, with most of the things we have to deal with. So, DO slow down and ask questions.

Personal Notes:

_____
_____
_____
_____
_____
_____
_____
_____
_____
_____
_____
_____
_____
_____
_____
_____
_____
_____
_____
_____
_____
_____
_____
_____
_____
_____

Devotion 53

Mordecai had come a long way, from an aged adoptive father, to a forgotten hero, to a man targeted for death, to the deliverer of his people. And all of that called for a change of clothes and headwear.

Esther 8:15 *And Mordecai went out from the presence of the king in royal apparel of blue and white, and with a great crown of gold, and with a garment of fine linen and purple: and the city of Shushan rejoiced and was glad. **16** The Jews had light, and gladness, and joy, and honour. **17** And in every province, and in every city, whithersoever the king's commandment and his decree came, the Jews had joy and gladness, a feast and a good day. And many of the people of the land became Jews; for the fear of the Jews fell upon them.*

That last phrase is of particular interest to me, "And many of the people of the land became Jews; for the fear of the Jews fell upon them." This is obviously not talking about ancestral descent; is talking about religious conversion. Many people who were not descended from Abraham, Isaac, and Jacob chose to convert to Judaism. And they did so specifically because of how powerful and successful the Jews had suddenly become. And while we may be inclined to scoff at such a "fair weather conversion," there is a very practical truth to be found within it, one that is still very applicable to our day and to

Christianity; people are drawn to that which is powerful, not to that which is pitiful.

Christians often develop the faulty belief that Christ expects us to be weak and pitiful and powerless and that somehow that will draw people to salvation. But the early church had thousands of members within just a few weeks' time and spread to every known corner of the world in just a few years' time. Furthermore, Paul, the main spokesman for Christianity, did not hesitate to flex his Roman rights when his life was threatened.

Were Christians often martyred? Certainly. Did they often have everything taken from them? Absolutely. And yet, those were circumstances, not commands! Jesus never said, "Be thou poverty-stricken, powerless, and pitiful." And if the early church and even Christians as a whole had been like that, Christianity likely would not have survived the first century.

DO "set your affection on things above" (Col. 3:2), but DO also be as successful as you can be here below!

Personal Notes:

_____
_____
_____
_____
_____
_____
_____

Devotion 54

Months passed, and finally, the day of Purim arrived. By now, everyone who wanted to kill Jews was prepared and ready to do so, and any Jews who wanted to live were prepared and ready to defend themselves. And then the day dawned, the bell rang, and the fight was on.

Esther 9:2 *The Jews gathered themselves together in their cities throughout all the provinces of the king Ahasuerus, to lay hand on such as sought their hurt: and no man could withstand them; for the fear of them fell upon all people. 3 And all the rulers of the provinces, and the lieutenants, and the deputies, and officers of the king, helped the Jews; because the fear of Mordecai fell upon them. 4 For Mordecai was great in the king's house, and his fame went out throughout all the provinces: for this man Mordecai waxed greater and greater. 5 Thus the Jews smote all their enemies with the stroke of the sword, and slaughter, and destruction, and did what they would unto those that hated them.*

It is incredible to realize that, even knowing that the king was in favor of the Jews, a battle to try and destroy them took place anyway. In fact, it is far more amazing than you may realize:

Esther 9:6 *And in Shushan the palace the Jews slew and destroyed five hundred men.*

Please remember that the second decree allowed the Jews to defend themselves. They were not the aggressors in any of this. How shocking is it, then, that right there in the palace, they had to kill five hundred men! Do you understand what that means? Esther was barricaded in her room, the king likely right there beside her, while savage anti-semites tried to get past security and murder her and Mordecai! Five hundred of them! Think back to what Mordecai warned her of when all of this started; in Esther 4:13 he told her specifically that she would not be safe even in the king's house.

Never underestimate the devil and his people's level of hatred toward anyone that God loves. DO be ready and prepared to deal with it!

Personal Notes:

_____
_____
_____
_____
_____
_____
_____
_____
_____
_____
_____
_____
_____
_____
_____
_____
_____
_____

Devotion 55

If you were to look into the encyclopedia for the phrase "smart lady," you may well find a picture of Esther under that heading.

Esther 9:12 *And the king said unto Esther the queen, The Jews have slain and destroyed five hundred men in Shushan the palace, and the ten sons of Haman; what have they done in the rest of the king's provinces? now what is thy petition? and it shall be granted thee: or what is thy request further? and it shall be done.* **13** *Then said Esther, If it please the king, let it be granted to the Jews which are in Shushan to do to morrow also according unto this day's decree, and let Haman's ten sons be hanged upon the gallows.*

The decree of Haman was for one single day. And yet, Esther asked for her decree, the decree allowing them to defend themselves, to extend for a second day. Now, why in the world would she do that? I mean, it's not like the devil's crowd would EVER hit someone after the bell has rung, right?

Esther 9:15 *For the Jews that were in Shushan gathered themselves together on the fourteenth day also of the month Adar, and slew three hundred men at Shushan; but on the prey they laid not their hand.*

Amazing... after losing five hundred men on the one day they were allowed to try and kill the Jews, they tried again the day after, in spite of the fact that they were not allowed to do so. The Jews had to kill another three hundred men a day after the decree was over in order to save Esther, Mordecai, and themselves.

Did you expect the devil to play by the rules? Has he ever been fair, even for a moment?

DO conduct yourself prudently, wisely, and carefully, as if the devil himself is going to try and break every rule to get to you – because he is!

Personal Notes:

_____

_____

_____

_____

_____

_____

_____

_____

_____

_____

_____

_____

_____

_____

_____

_____

_____

_____

_____

_____

Devotion 56

In all of this that surrounded Purim, there is a big small thing that often goes overlooked.

Esther 9:15 *For the Jews that were in Shushan gathered themselves together on the fourteenth day also of the month Adar, and slew three hundred men at Shushan; but on the prey they laid not their hand.* **16** *But the other Jews that were in the king's provinces gathered themselves together, and stood for their lives, and had rest from their enemies, and slew of their foes seventy and five thousand, but they laid not their hands on the prey,*

In two straight verses, we are told that they did not lay their hands on the prey, meaning that even though they killed those who were trying to kill them, they did not take so much as one penny or item that belonged to them.

They were specifically allowed to do so:

Esther 8:11 *Wherein the king granted the Jews which were in every city to gather themselves together, and to stand for their life, to destroy, to slay, and to cause to perish, all the power of the people and province that would assault them, both little ones and women, and to take the spoil of them for a prey,*

It is breathtaking that hundreds of thousands of Jews defended themselves and killed their enemies, yet not one of them took any prey though all of them were allowed to! How does such a thing happen, and why? It happens when people realize that not everything that is allowed is actually a good idea and that a good name is more important than untold wealth. Throughout the centuries, the Jewish people have always been accused of being money-grubbing, underhanded thieves, yet when they had the wealth of their enemies handed to them on a silver platter, they declined it all. They knew that the whole world was watching, wondering why they had been allowed to be targeted and if maybe there was a good reason for it. By simply defending themselves and doing nothing else, they built a testimony of honesty and honorability that would never be easily discredited.

DO guard your testimony!

Personal Notes:

_____

_____

_____

_____

_____

_____

_____

_____

_____

_____

_____

_____

_____

_____

_____

_____

_____

Devotion 57

After two days of fighting in Shushan the palace and one day of fighting throughout the rest of the Empire, the Jews knew that by God's good grace and the efforts of Esther and Mordecai, they were now safe. And that is how a potential day of disaster turned into one of the longest-standing holidays in Earth's history.

Esther 9:19 *Therefore the Jews of the villages, that dwelt in the unwalled towns, made the fourteenth day of the month Adar a day of gladness and feasting, and a good day, and of sending portions one to another.* **20** *And Mordecai wrote these things, and sent letters unto all the Jews that were in all the provinces of the king Ahasuerus, both nigh and far,* **21** *To stablish this among them, that they should keep the fourteenth day of the month Adar, and the fifteenth day of the same, yearly,* **22** *As the days wherein the Jews rested from their enemies, and the month which was turned unto them from sorrow to joy, and from mourning into a good day: that they should make them days of feasting and joy, and of sending portions one to another, and gifts to the poor.*

Every year in early spring, you will find the word Purim on your calendar. For nearly 2500 years, the Jews have been celebrating this wonderful day. We read here that from the very first celebration of it, it was to include feasting and joy and gifts both to those they loved and also to the poor. Purim is an excellent forerunner to everything that we do at Christmas!

It is wonderfully appropriate to have joyful holidays, despite the fact that from time to time, you will meet modern Haman/Grinches who do not like it. And while the law would certainly frown on it if you hang them from a gallows before you go on with your celebration, you may most certainly hang their stuffy and miserable opinions out to dry before you do so! When God does great things, a celebration should be our logical choice.

DO enjoy the holidays. Or, as Tiny Tim might have put it if he had lived through Purim, "And God bless us, everyone... except for Haman."

Personal Notes:

_____
_____
_____
_____
_____
_____
_____
_____
_____
_____
_____
_____
_____
_____
_____
_____

Devotion 58

The entire last chapter of the book of Esther is just a short three verses. But it is a loaded short three verses.

Esther 10:1 *And the king Ahasuerus laid a tribute upon the land, and upon the isles of the sea.* 2 *And all the acts of his power and of his might, and the declaration of the greatness of Mordecai, whereunto the king advanced him, are they not written in the book of the chronicles of the kings of Media and Persia?* 3 *For Mordecai the Jew was next unto king Ahasuerus, and great among the Jews, and accepted of the multitude of his brethren, seeking the wealth of his people, and speaking peace to all his seed.*

Mordecai was a Jew. And yet he was written about glowingly in the book of the Chronicles of the Kings of Media and Persia. But if you look at a world map today, you will not find Persia on it. The landmass is still there, obviously. The people are still there. And it maintained the name of Persia for a very long time after Mordecai's day, around 2,300 years. But in 1935, the name Persia, that elegant name full of history, gave way to a different name – Iran. And then, in 1979, Iran underwent a revolution and became a hard-line Islamic theocracy. From that moment on, they have sought to destroy the Jews with all of their might.

Their greatest queen was a Jew. Their greatest right-hand man to a king was a Jew.

How often mankind forgets the good things that others have done for them! And it is wrong every time that happens. If there is anything that we should ever keep a long memory for, it is the kindnesses of others, especially when they have never done anything to undermine those kindnesses. The Jews never gave Persia/Iran any reason to hate them, only and always gave them reason to respect them, and yet are now their most despised target.

DO have a long memory for the kindnesses of others!

Personal Notes:

_____
_____
_____
_____
_____
_____
_____
_____
_____
_____
_____
_____
_____
_____
_____
_____
_____
_____
_____

Devotion 59

Job 1:1 *There was a man in the land of Uz, whose name was Job; and that man was perfect and upright, and one that feared God, and eschewed evil.* **2** *And there were born unto him seven sons and three daughters.* **3** *His substance also was seven thousand sheep, and three thousand camels, and five hundred yoke of oxen, and five hundred she asses, and a very great household; so that this man was the greatest of all the men of the east.*

The book of Job is one of the most unique books in the Bible. Indeed, it is one of the most unique books on earth! It begins the books of poetry in the Bible (Job-Song of Solomon), and yet, it begins and ends in prose. The first two chapters and the last ten verses are prose; everything sandwiched in between is Hebrew poetry. And yet that poetry is an inspired, true, accurate, word-for-word account of all that took place.

Job is widely regarded as one of the oldest writings in human history. Job himself seems to have lived prior to Abraham, so we are beginning to look at the account of a man who lived probably 4,000 years ago or longer.

As we are introduced to him, in addition to his great wealth, we are told that he was "perfect and upright, and one that feared God, and eschewed evil." And it is that, his morality rather than his money, that made him a target of Satan in this book.

If you really want to cause the devil grief, please be aware that getting rich is not the way to do it. Satan does not care if you become the wealthiest human being that has ever lived. Nor does God, by the way. But both the devil and God care very deeply when and if you choose to live right, especially if you do so to such a degree that God himself calls you a perfect and an upright person.

Life is too short and eternity is too long for us to slide along under both God's radar and the devil's radar; DO make yourself known, DO live right in a world that lives wrong!

Personal Notes:

_____

_____

_____

_____

_____

_____

_____

_____

_____

_____

_____

_____

_____

_____

_____

_____

_____

_____

_____

Devotion 60

After being introduced to Job, we are quickly introduced to Job's family. And we see right away that they were something very enviable; they were a close, tight-knit family.

Job 1:4 *And his sons went and feasted in their houses, every one his day; and sent and called for their three sisters to eat and to drink with them.*

Job had ten children: seven sons and three daughters. Each time a birthday came around, all of the brothers and all of the sisters came to celebrate it. Just think about that; how likely is it that in a family with ten children, all of them get along that incredibly well? Job truly was a blessed man.

But he was also an insightful man. He knew the human character and made no assumptions about the righteousness of his children:

Job 1:5 *And it was so, when the days of their feasting were gone about, that Job sent and sanctified them, and rose up early in the morning, and offered burnt offerings according to the number of them all: for Job said, It may be that my sons have sinned, and cursed God in their hearts. Thus did Job continually.*

When the last birthday of the year was done, Job gathered all of his children together and offered a sacrifice for each one just in case any of them had sinned, even an unseen sin such as cursing God in their hearts. Job, in other words, was not satisfied that he alone be regarded as a perfect and an upright man before God. He intended for all of his children to understand matters of righteousness and to follow in his footsteps.

Can you imagine the impression that made on his children each and every year?

Moms and dads, things like gathering your children together and praying out loud over them make a powerful impression. DO make your walk with the Lord an open, visible, familial thing!

Personal Notes:

_____
_____
_____
_____
_____
_____
_____
_____
_____
_____
_____
_____
_____
_____
_____
_____
_____
_____
_____
_____
_____

Devotion 61

Into the narrative of Job and his family now enters a malevolent presence, and the book will take a sharp turn when he does.

Job 1:6 *Now there was a day when the sons of God came to present themselves before the LORD, and Satan came also among them.*

There has been much needless debate as to who these sons of God are in this verse. The reason it is needless is because this very book spells it out for us clearly.

Job 38:4 *Where wast thou when I laid the foundations of the earth? declare, if thou hast understanding.* **5** *Who hath laid the measures thereof, if thou knowest? or who hath stretched the line upon it?* **6** *Whereupon are the foundations thereof fastened? or who laid the corner stone thereof;* **7** *When the morning stars sang together, and all the sons of God shouted for joy?*

This is God speaking of the time when He first made the earth, before He even created man. At that point, the "sons of God" shouted for joy. Clearly, then, these are angelic beings. And that means that as we examine Job 1:6, we are to learn that those mighty creatures, fallen and unfallen, must regularly present themselves before the Lord to answer for their doings. Mind you, it isn't like the omniscient God doesn't know; it is that as God, everything and everyone must answer to Him for the things that He already knows.

Even Satan himself had to come and present himself for this purpose.

And that provides us with a joyful bit of necessary theology before we get to the brokenness and bitterness of the book; Satan cannot just do whatever he wants and get by with it. He has limitations imposed upon him by God Himself and must answer for his deeds within those limitations.

On those days that you begin to feel like the devil cannot be beaten, DO remember that while he is a lion, he is a lion on a leash!

Personal Notes:

_____
_____
_____
_____
_____
_____
_____
_____
_____
_____
_____
_____
_____
_____
_____
_____
_____
_____
_____
_____

Devotion 62

When it came time for Satan to answer to God, the conversation very quickly became interesting, as you might expect.

Job 1:7 *And the LORD said unto Satan, Whence comest thou? Then Satan answered the LORD, and said, From going to and fro in the earth, and from walking up and down in it.* **8** *And the LORD said unto Satan, Hast thou considered my servant Job, that there is none like him in the earth, a perfect and an upright man, one that feareth God, and escheweth evil?* **9** *Then Satan answered the LORD, and said, Doth Job fear God for nought?* **10** *Hast not thou made an hedge about him, and about his house, and about all that he hath on every side? thou hast blessed the work of his hands, and his substance is increased in the land.*

For the second time, we find Job described as a "*perfect and an upright man, one that feareth God, and escheweth* [rejects and turns away from] *evil,*" and it is God Himself who gives him that description. But something equally stunning we find is that when God asked the devil if he had considered Job, we find very clearly that he had done much more than just consider him; he had looked at him under a microscope and knew everything about him! He knew that Job feared God, he knew that there was a divine hedge about him and his house, and he knew about Job's work and wealth.

When it boils right down to it, we, as children of God, are going to have to take one of two approaches concerning the devil. We can either try to sneak quietly past him from day to day and hope he doesn't notice us, or we can live so fully and openly for God each day that he cannot possibly miss us! And before you think, "Well, based on what he went through, option one doesn't sound so bad!" please remember that time is very short... and eternity is infinitely long.

DO antagonize the devil every single day by living for God; God likes it, the devil hates it, and you will have a lot more interesting things to reminisce about while sitting on the front porch of a mansion in heaven!

Personal Notes:

_____
_____
_____
_____
_____
_____
_____
_____
_____
_____
_____
_____
_____

Devotion 63

One question almost always gets asked about the book of Job: why do bad things happen to good people like that? But a question that does not get asked, but should, is "What was the devil's motivation for all of this?"

The good news about that question is that it has a clear and specific answer. Not once, but twice, Satan specifically spelled it out for us.

Job 1:11 *But put forth thine hand now, and touch all that he hath, and he will curse thee to thy face.*

Job 2:5 *But put forth thine hand now, and touch his bone and his flesh, and he will curse thee to thy face.*

Satan's goal was to prove to God that Job only loved him because God was giving him what he wanted, and if God ever did not give him what he wanted, Job would actually go so far as to openly defy Him, cursing Him to His face! Throughout this book, in ways seen and unseen, that was consistently what the devil tried (very unsuccessfully) to bring about.

Now, what in the world would ever give the devil the idea that if someone did not get what they wanted, they would go so far as to curse God to His face? The answer to that one is pretty obvious, isn't it? He himself had once joyfully worshiped God, and then, when God would not give up His throne for him, became His fiercest enemy, constantly cursing Him and motivating others to do the same.

In other words, this was the devil's attempt to prove to God that what he did and has done is perfectly reasonable. He believes it is normal for people to only "love" God when He gives them whatever they want. Job, though, proved him wrong in dramatic fashion. The question, though, is whether or not we will prove him wrong in our own lives.

DO love God for God; a love of God that is dependent on God always giving us all of the desires of our heart is no love at all!

Personal Notes:

_____

_____

_____

_____

_____

_____

_____

_____

_____

_____

_____

_____

_____

_____

_____

_____

_____

_____

_____

Devotion 64

Satan had challenged God concerning the love of Job. His assertion was that Job would curse God to His face if God took everything that he had. And here is how God answered:

Job 1:12 *And the LORD said unto Satan, Behold, all that he hath is in thy power; only upon himself put not forth thine hand. So Satan went forth from the presence of the LORD.*

I want you to compare the words of this verse with the words of the verse just previous to it very carefully:

Job 1:11 *But put forth thine hand now, and touch all that he hath, and he will curse thee to thy face.*

Do you see it? The devil asked God to put His hand out and touch Job, taking everything from him. God's answer was that Satan had permission to put his own hand out and do so. Throughout this book, Job makes the mistake over and over again of assuming that God took everything from him.

God took nothing from him. The devil did it all.

This is not splitting theological hairs. Yes, God allowed it, but no, God did not do it. Senseless evil will always be sourced from a senseless evil being, never from the good God who made us. If Job had grasped that, his trials would have still been agonizing, but he would not have had to bear the extra weight of his trials also seeming to be an assault from the God he had loved and served so faithfully.

When senseless things come into your life, hurts and attacks and evils that make no sense, DO look carefully at the handprints on them because you will always find claw marks instead of the marks of the hands that were pierced for you.

Personal Notes:

_____
_____
_____
_____
_____
_____
_____
_____
_____
_____
_____
_____
_____
_____
_____
_____
_____
_____
_____
_____
_____
_____
_____
_____

Devotion 65

We now come to the greatest series of tragedies any man has ever known.

Job 1:13 *And there was a day when his sons and his daughters were eating and drinking wine in their eldest brother's house:* **14** *And there came a messenger unto Job, and said, The oxen were plowing, and the asses feeding beside them:* **15** *And the Sabeans fell upon them, and took them away; yea, they have slain the servants with the edge of the sword; and I only am escaped alone to tell thee.* **16** *While he was yet speaking, there came also another, and said, The fire of God is fallen from heaven, and hath burned up the sheep, and the servants, and consumed them; and I only am escaped alone to tell thee.* **17** *While he was yet speaking, there came also another, and said, The Chaldeans made out three bands, and fell upon the camels, and have carried them away, yea, and slain the servants with the edge of the sword; and I only am escaped alone to tell thee.* **18** *While he was yet speaking, there came also another, and said, Thy sons and thy daughters were eating and drinking wine in their eldest brother's house:* **19** *And, behold, there came a great wind from the wilderness, and smote the four corners of the house, and it fell upon the young men, and they are dead; and I only am escaped alone to tell thee.*

Satan is evil, but he is also very good at what he does. Four separate attacks were leveled simultaneously. The oxen and asses were taken, the sheep were burned up with fire from the sky, the camels were taken, and then a great wind leveled a house and killed all ten of the children. But in each case, all of the servants were killed except one, one who could run and tell Job what happened. And the messengers arrived in such a way that they left no time between their messages for Job to get his wind back. The last one, naturally, was the word about the death of his children.

All of this was designed for maximum impact. Satan was trying to crush this man.

But he couldn't do it.

Child of God, DO look at Job and realize that God has built into you the strength you will need to withstand the attacks of the devil. The devil may be allowed to put his hand on you, but God will never take HIS hand off of you!

Personal Notes:

_____

_____

_____

_____

_____

_____

_____

_____

_____

_____

_____

Devotion 66

Word of the multi-faceted tragedy had reached Job. The devil was expecting him to curse God in response. But instead, this is what he got:

Job 1:20 *Then Job arose, and rent his mantle, and shaved his head, and fell down upon the ground, and worshipped,* **21** *And said, Naked came I out of my mother's womb, and naked shall I return thither: the LORD gave, and the LORD hath taken away; blessed be the name of the LORD.* **22** *In all this Job sinned not, nor charged God foolishly.*

We have already pointed out that Job got one part of this wrong. The Lord did indeed give, but it was not the Lord who took away. The devil did that. Nonetheless, all of his other theology and understanding of the subject were correct. All of us do come into this world with nothing, and all of us leave with nothing. Because Job understood this, rather than cursing the Lord, he said, "Blessed be the name of the Lord."

But is the information we are given in verse twenty that I find to be normally overlooked yet utterly fascinating. Job got up. Job tore his mantle. Then Job shaved his head. And then he fell down on the ground and worshipped. In other words, none of this was quick. Especially the shaving of the head would have taken a while. Job chose not to react, not to say anything until he had taken the time to do those other things so symbolic of mourning.

When hurts and pains and even tragedies happen, haste is generally our enemy rather than our ally. Yes, Job did not curse the Lord because he loved the Lord, but it is clear that he also did not curse the Lord because he did not speak immediately; he took time to gather himself first.

The devil may sometimes be given control over what comes into our lives, but he is never given control over what comes out of our mouths and how soon it does so. DO take the time in every circumstance to prepare yourself to speak rightly!

Personal Notes:

_____
_____
_____
_____
_____
_____
_____
_____
_____
_____
_____
_____
_____
_____
_____
_____
_____
_____
_____

Devotion 67

Round one of the battle over Job was now done, and round two was about to commence.

Job 2:1 *Again there was a day when the sons of God came to present themselves before the LORD, and Satan came also among them to present himself before the LORD.* **2** *And the LORD said unto Satan, From whence comest thou? And Satan answered the LORD, and said, From going to and fro in the earth, and from walking up and down in it.* **3** *And the LORD said unto Satan, Hast thou considered my servant Job, that there is none like him in the earth, a perfect and an upright man, one that feareth God, and escheweth evil? and still he holdeth fast his integrity, although thou movedst me against him, to destroy him without cause.*

When God and Satan spoke the first time, God was able to describe Job as a perfect and an upright man, one that feared God and eschewed evil. But now, He was able to add an extra phrase, "*and still he holdeth fast his integrity, although thou movedst me against him, to destroy him without cause.*" In other words, God had previously been able to speak of the uprightness of Job, but He had never been able to speak of the devotion of Job. You see, devotion is not revealed during the times when everything is going right in our lives; it is revealed during the times when everything is going wrong in our lives.

Serving God with full cupboards and loaded bank accounts and healthy bodies and secure families is right but says nothing about our devotion.

When the hard times come, and they ultimately will, DO view that as the time to demonstrate your devotion. DO give God something enjoyable to talk about when it comes to you!

Personal Notes:

_____
_____
_____
_____
_____
_____
_____
_____
_____
_____
_____
_____
_____
_____
_____
_____
_____
_____
_____
_____
_____
_____
_____
_____

Devotion 68

Satan had previously asserted that if Job's possessions were taken, he would curse God to His face. But Job had shattered that assertion. So, in round two, Satan would change his terms:

Job 2:4 *And Satan answered the Lord, and said, Skin for skin, yea, all that a man hath will he give for his life.* **5** *But put forth thine hand now, and touch his bone and his flesh, and he will curse thee to thy face.*

It is clear that Satan had a very low view of mankind. But truthfully, he had a lot of evidence to support his assertion! Even all the way up into the book of the Revelation, look what we find:

Revelation 16:9 *And men were scorched with great heat, and blasphemed the name of God, which hath power over these plagues: and they repented not to give him glory.*

That is exactly what Satan was describing. His mistake, though, was assuming that Job was just like most everyone else. But Job was different, and you and I can be too. We may be descended from Adam and from our parents and grandparents, but we are not them. We all have the right and ability to choose a better way; we all have the ability to prove the devil wrong.

DO prove him wrong!

Personal Notes:

Devotion 69

Round two of the trial of Job was about to begin, and it was going to be brutal.

Job 2:6 *And the LORD said unto Satan, Behold, he is in thine hand; but save his life.* **7** *So went Satan forth from the presence of the LORD, and smote Job with sore boils from the sole of his foot unto his crown.*

This attack of Satan was designed to inflict maximum physical and mental torture upon Job. This was not something that was going to make Job die; this was something that was going to make Job wish that he could die. It was Satan's second attempt to get Job to curse God, and a dead person cannot do that.

With Job's body covered in boils from the top of his head to the bottom of his feet, absolutely everything hurt. Standing or sitting or lying hurt. Eating or not eating hurt. Drinking or not drinking hurt. This was sheer agony every single second of the day and night in a day when there was no medication available to even begin to alleviate the pain. But what Job did have was a most unlikely source of comfort:

Job 2:8 *And he took him a potsherd to scrape himself withal; and he sat down among the ashes.*

Sometime before all of this happened, a piece of pottery had broken. And for whatever reason, Job decided to save a piece of that broken pottery. And now, in his greatest hour of need, he was able to use that broken pottery to scrape the boils and give himself a small measure of relief. I can almost see the devil smacking his forehead and saying, "Well, I didn't see that coming!"

And yet, how often is it in our own lives that the "broken things" of our past are the very things that God uses in some way to bring comfort in our present agony?

DO be slow to despise "broken things." The God who knows our future may have had a very good reason to let them break!

Personal Notes:

_____

_____

_____

_____

_____

_____

_____

_____

_____

_____

_____

_____

_____

_____

_____

_____

_____

_____

_____

_____

_____

_____

Devotion 70

We now arrive at one of the most gut-wrenching portions of the book of Job, a time when a brokenhearted mother's words finally came tumbling out.

Job 2:9 *Then said his wife unto him, Dost thou still retain thine integrity? curse God, and die.* **10** *But he said unto her, Thou speakest as one of the foolish women speaketh. What? shall we receive good at the hand of God, and shall we not receive evil? In all this did not Job sin with his lips.*

I am not minimizing what Job's wife did and said here. I understand that, though she obviously did not know it, she was actually directly playing into the devil's hands, trying to get her husband to do the very thing that Satan told God he would do. But let us please remind ourselves that this dear lady is still dealing with the devastating loss of all ten of her children all at once. And now, her husband cannot even put his arms around her to hug and comfort her because of all the boils all over his body.

Yes, Job suffered like no man ever suffered, but Job's wife suffered like no woman ever suffered.

Job was right to call her down for what she said. He was her husband. But anyone else today sitting in their comfortable home with all of their family healthy and intact should tread very lightly at this passage and keep any uncharitable opinions of Job's wife entirely to themselves, I think.

That said, there are a couple of things to learn from this. One, DO be aware that in times of deep hurt, you are going to be tempted to say things you should not say. Two, DO stand ready to keep everything and everyone right, even in times of deep hurt. Never let trials become the fertile soil of transgression!

Personal Notes:

_____

_____

_____

_____

_____

_____

_____

_____

_____

_____

_____

_____

_____

_____

_____

_____

_____

_____

_____

_____

_____

_____

Devotion 71

Thus far in the book of Job, we have seen God, Satan, Job, his wife, a few servants, and ten children now deceased. But now some new characters will enter the narrative, and though they are not related to Job and have not experienced any of the tragedy, they will take up the bulk of the rest of the book.

Job 2:11 *Now when Job's three friends heard of all this evil that was come upon him, they came every one from his own place; Eliphaz the Temanite, and Bildad the Shuhite, and Zophar the Naamathite: for they had made an appointment together to come to mourn with him and to comfort him.* **12** *And when they lifted up their eyes afar off, and knew him not, they lifted up their voice, and wept; and they rent every one his mantle, and sprinkled dust upon their heads toward heaven.* **13** *So they sat down with him upon the ground seven days and seven nights, and none spake a word unto him: for they saw that his grief was very great.*

Anyone who knows the book of Job knows that these men, from this point forward, absolutely blow it. They managed to do the unthinkable, making Job's plight even worse. But at this point in the text, they actually give a textbook example of what to do when someone you know is grieving. Here are some of the particulars. They came. They made an appointment, and all came together. They cried with him. They said nothing. They sat quietly with him for a long time.

Everything about that pattern is lovely. It showed effort and planning and true compassion, and it did not come across as trite and shallow, as most things said at such a time do. When people are hurting like this, you cannot make it better, but you can sit with them as they take their next breath and their next and their next. And if you do, you will be helping them to take those next breaths.

When you want to help someone who is hurting, DO keep it as simple as possible!

Personal Notes:

_____
_____
_____
_____
_____
_____
_____
_____
_____
_____
_____
_____
_____
_____
_____
_____
_____
_____
_____

Devotion 72

Let me tell you how most people view the book of Job. Job 1-2: "HUGE DRAMA! THE DEVIL ATTACKS JOB!" Job 38-42: "HUGE DRAMA! GOD SPEAKS TO JOB OUT OF THE WHIRLWIND!" Job 3-37: "Ho-hum, people talking about stuff, and then some other stuff, yawn..."

But those neglected chapters are, in a sense, the entire point of the book. They are a debate between Job and his friends about the very nature and character of God. As such, they are incredibly valuable. And here is how that thirty-five-chapter discussion began.

Job 3:1 *After this opened Job his mouth, and cursed his day.* **2** *And Job spake, and said,* **3** *Let the day perish wherein I was born, and the night in which it was said, There is a man child conceived.* **4** *Let that day be darkness; let not God regard it from above, neither let the light shine upon it.* **5** *Let darkness and the shadow of death stain it; let a cloud dwell upon it; let the blackness of the day terrify it.* **6** *As for that night, let darkness seize upon it; let it not be joined unto the days of the year, let it not come into the number of the months.*

In all of those words, Job was clearly saying, "I wish I had never been born." And yet it was his very first words that must have been so galling to Satan. Job "cursed his day," meaning the day he was born.

148

That is not what Satan was after. He was trying to get Job to curse God; instead, Job merely cursed the day he was born. And then he went on in verse four to speak of God above. To Job, there was a big difference between despising God and despising circumstances. And that is a valuable distinction to make.

DO revere God even when you revile circumstances!

Personal Notes:

_____

_____

_____

_____

_____

_____

_____

_____

_____

_____

_____

_____

_____

_____

_____

_____

_____

_____

_____

Devotion 73

As Job continued his opening words of complaint, words that most people simply skim over, he gives us another reason not to pass them by lightly, another treasure of truth:

Job 3:11 *Why died I not from the womb? why did I not give up the ghost when I came out of the belly?* **12** *Why did the knees prevent me? or why the breasts that I should suck?* **13** *For now should I have lain still and been quiet, I should have slept: then had I been at rest,* **14** *With kings and counsellors of the earth, which built desolate places for themselves;* **15** *Or with princes that had gold, who filled their houses with silver:* **16** *Or as an hidden untimely birth I had not been; as infants which never saw light.* **17** *There the wicked cease from troubling; and there the weary be at rest.*

In verses eleven and twelve, Job asked four questions, all of which meant, "Why could I have not died during birth?" In verse sixteen, he backed that up a bit further and asked why he could not have been miscarried. But his reasoning for that desire was that in both cases, he would be at rest along with people who had lived full lives and then died.

Not "gone," at rest. This is clear Biblical teaching that babies are living souls, and even if they never even make it out of the womb alive, they go straight to heaven when they die.

Job went through very much. And yet one of the beautiful, comforting things that came out of it is this precious assurance to parents of every generation to follow, including ours.

DO know that if you lost a child like that, you didn't really lose them; they are just waiting for you to arrive!

Personal Notes:

_____
_____
_____
_____
_____
_____
_____
_____
_____
_____
_____
_____
_____
_____
_____
_____
_____
_____
_____
_____
_____
_____

Devotion 74

We often ask the question, "What was he/she thinking?" Most of the time, we do not get the answer to that. But in the case of Job and his trials, Job, at the end of his first complaint, lets us know what he had been thinking prior to his calamities.

Job 3:24 *For my sighing cometh before I eat, and my roarings are poured out like the waters.* **25** *For the thing which I greatly feared is come upon me, and that which I was afraid of is come unto me.* **26** *I was not in safety, neither had I rest, neither was I quiet; yet trouble came.*

Job said in verse twenty-five, "*The thing which I greatly feared is come upon me, and that which I was afraid of is come unto me.*" In other words, even before anything happened, he had been dreading the possibility of all of this happening! And then, in verse twenty-six, he adds, "*I was not in safety, neither had I rest, neither was I quiet; yet trouble came.*" Those words mean that, even while he was successful and healthy and nothing was wrong, he was living life as cautiously as if he was every moment walking on eggshells.

I hope you understand how bad of a thing all of that is! Job was causing himself untold mental and emotional anguish before anything ever actually went wrong! So, even if he had lived from the cradle to the grave without any of this happening, he still would have had high blood pressure, stress headaches, and a host of other nervous disorders as the years wore on!

Yes, Job was a perfect and an upright man. But no, Job was not a good example to follow when it comes to worry!

None of you would knowingly let a destroyer in your home. And yet, so very many actually do just that, welcoming worry 24/7/365. What a miserable way to live.

DO be wise, do take as many sensible precautions as you can, but DO NOT allow worry to make you as miserable as if all of your imagined calamities are actually real!

Personal Notes:

_____
_____
_____
_____
_____
_____
_____
_____
_____
_____
_____
_____
_____
_____
_____
_____
_____
_____

Devotion 75

After Job finished his first complaint, Eliphaz, of all things, decided to argue with it.

Job 4:1 *Then Eliphaz the Temanite answered and said,* **2** *If we assay to commune with thee, wilt thou be grieved? but who can withhold himself from speaking?* **3** *Behold, thou hast instructed many, and thou hast strengthened the weak hands.* **4** *Thy words have upholden him that was falling, and thou hast strengthened the feeble knees.* **5** *But now it is come upon thee, and thou faintest; it toucheth thee, and thou art troubled.* **6** *Is not this thy fear, thy confidence, thy hope, and the uprightness of thy ways?* **7** *Remember, I pray thee, who ever perished, being innocent? or where were the righteous cut off?* **8** *Even as I have seen, they that plow iniquity, and sow wickedness, reap the same.*

Eliphaz was of the stated opinion that no innocent person ever perished, and no righteous person was ever cut off. His view was that only those who "plow iniquity" and "sow wickedness" ever experience that.

It's almost like he never heard of a guy named Abel.

Job will deal with that argument pretty thoroughly, reiterating the truth that I just stated. Oftentimes, the righteous are, in fact, cut off!

But it is the question Eliphaz asked in verse two that I want to deal with for a moment. He said,

"Who can withhold himself from speaking?" And the answer to that is, "YOU can, Pal!" This notion that people absolutely, positively have to speak up each and every time they hear or see something they do not like is pure arrogance. For instance, the "preacher" who recently drove onto the campus of a Christian college and videotaped girls dressed more modestly than he liked and posted it, mocking them and the college.

That is some industrial-grade pervert material.

Every one of us has the ability to simply pass by things without having to comment on them. DO make liberal use of that ability!

Personal Notes:

_____

_____

_____

_____

_____

_____

_____

_____

_____

_____

_____

_____

_____

_____

_____

_____

_____

_____

_____

Devotion 76

Eliphaz was VERY sure of himself and his belief that Job was wicked and being punished by God for his sin. So, what was his source of information? Be ready to bang your head on the table...

Job 4:12 *Now a thing was secretly brought to me, and mine ear received a little thereof.* **13** *In thoughts from the visions of the night, when deep sleep falleth on men,* **14** *Fear came upon me, and trembling, which made all my bones to shake.* **15** *Then a spirit passed before my face; the hair of my flesh stood up:* **16** *It stood still, but I could not discern the form thereof: an image was before mine eyes, there was silence, and I heard a voice, saying,* **17** *Shall mortal man be more just than God? shall a man be more pure than his maker?*

A ghost. Dude is literally ripping his hurting friend to shreds because he got top-secret intel from a GHOST.

His bones were shaking... and the hairs on his arms stood up!

Well, now, if that doesn't just settle the issue!

Job should have given him a nuclear wedgie.

In all seriousness, though, this goes to show why any "personal revelation" is not to be trusted, whether it comes from an ancient guy who saw a ghost or a top-selling author that God keeps "speaking to" and saying things that directly contradict everything His Word says about sin. Especially now that we have the completed, written revelation of God to man, the Bible, DO know exactly where to put any "personal revelation," namely in the garbage bin!

Personal Notes:

_____

_____

_____

_____

_____

_____

_____

_____

_____

_____

_____

_____

_____

_____

_____

_____

_____

_____

_____

_____

_____

_____

_____

_____

_____

Devotion 77

As Eliphaz continues his diatribe into chapter five, he gets ever more verbose and arrogant and even hurtful in his words.

Job 5:1 *Call now, if there be any that will answer thee; and to which of the saints wilt thou turn?* **2** *For wrath killeth the foolish man, and envy slayeth the silly one.* **3** *I have seen the foolish taking root: but suddenly I cursed his habitation.* **4** *His children are far from safety, and they are crushed in the gate, neither is there any to deliver them.*

Let us, first of all, examine the insults and brutal stabbing words Eliphaz just delivered to his hurting friend.

He began by strongly inferring that Job was foolish and silly. And yet, as is so often the case with know-it-alls, he contradicted his own previous word in all of this:

Job 4:3 *Behold, thou hast instructed many, and thou hast strengthened the weak hands.*

So, which is it, Eliphaz? Has Job instructed many, or is he foolish and silly?

But then he got infinitely worse, saying, "*His children are far from safety, and they are crushed in the gate, neither is there any to deliver them.*" All ten of Job's children died all at once, and Eliphaz is hitting him with this, the accusation that his children died because he, Job, was a foolish and silly man rather than a godly and righteous man! Can you even imagine this? "Hey, my brother in Christ, I just wanted you to know that God killed all of your children because you are a horrible person."

He began, though, with "to which of the saints wilt thou turn?" In other words, "Who (Abel) will (Noah) ever agree (Isaac) that you are suffering (Joseph) while doing right?"

DO understand that disaster is no proof of sin, nor is prosperity proof of righteousness!

Personal Notes:

_____

_____

_____

_____

_____

_____

_____

_____

_____

_____

_____

_____

_____

_____

_____

_____

_____

_____

_____

_____

_____

Devotion 78

After telling Job that his children were dead because of his foolishness, Eliphaz decided that he should next tell Job how to "fix the problem."

Job 5:8 *I would seek unto God, and unto God would I commit my cause:* **9** *Which doeth great things and unsearchable; marvellous things without number:* **10** *Who giveth rain upon the earth, and sendeth waters upon the fields:* **11** *To set up on high those that be low; that those which mourn may be exalted to safety.*

Eliphaz looked at his friend, who had lost every bit of his wealth and sustenance, all ten of his children, and was in indescribable physical agony every moment of the day and night, and said, "You know, if I were in your place, I would talk to God about this."

Gee, thanks, pal; I never would've thought of that.

There seems to be this natural tendency, even among believers, to want to oversimplify things that make us uncomfortable. "Job has been devastated. Therefore, he must not have been praying." And yet we know from God's own description of Job that that was not the case.

All of us live in a broken world. And to make matters worse, all of us have an active, voracious enemy, the devil. Because of that, even the righteous are often going to suffer. Actually, it will probably be more accurate to say ESPECIALLY the righteous are going to suffer since we are going to be his primary targets! Because of that, we need to be very careful not to put convenient religious Band-Aids like "Praying would fix this" on problems that we do not even understand.

DO pray because it does make a difference in everything, one way or another. But DO NOT assume someone has not been praying because of how badly things are going for them, and definitely DO NOT brush someone's problems off with a calloused, "You just need to pray!"

Personal Notes:

_____

_____

_____

_____

_____

_____

_____

_____

_____

_____

_____

_____

_____

_____

_____

_____

_____

_____

_____

Devotion 79

As Eliphaz continued his diatribe against Job, he got to something "almost scriptural."

Job 5:17 *Behold, happy is the man whom God correcteth: therefore despise not thou the chastening of the Almighty:* **18** *For he maketh sore, and bindeth up: he woundeth, and his hands make whole.* **19** *He shall deliver thee in six troubles: yea, in seven there shall no evil touch thee.* **20** *In famine he shall redeem thee from death: and in war from the power of the sword.* **21** *Thou shalt be hid from the scourge of the tongue: neither shalt thou be afraid of destruction when it cometh.*

If that statement, *"happy is the man whom God correcteth: therefore despise not thou the chastening of the Almighty,"* seems familiar, it is because both Solomon in the book of Proverbs and the writer of Hebrews many generations later wrote very similar words. In fact, similar things to everything that Eliphaz said from verses eighteen through twenty-one can also be found throughout Scripture.

But the reason this only qualifies as "almost scriptural" is for the exact same reason no one gets excited about teeing off on the first hole and seeing the ball slice so dramatically that it ends up landing in the cup on the fourth hole. It may be in the cup, but it isn't a hole-in-one if it isn't even on the right green!

Job was not being chastened. Job was not being corrected. Job was being tormented at the hands of the devil, period. Therefore, all of Eliphaz's assertions were wrong when applied to Job. God never once used that term in regard to Job. In the entire book, in fact, Eliphaz is the only one to ever use it!

Right things attached in the wrong places become wrong things. This is why one of the dumbest things any of us can ever do is make assumptions.

In any spiritually troubling situation, DO find out all of the details BEFORE you start trying to apply solutions!

Personal Notes:

_____

_____

_____

_____

_____

_____

_____

_____

_____

_____

_____

_____

_____

_____

_____

_____

_____

Devotion 80

Eliphaz was wrapping up his first diatribe against Job, so he decided to tell Job what things would be like if Job were only "smart enough" to follow his advice.

Job 5:21 *Thou shalt be hid from the scourge of the tongue: neither shalt thou be afraid of destruction when it cometh.* **22** *At destruction and famine thou shalt laugh: neither shalt thou be afraid of the beasts of the earth.* **23** *For thou shalt be in league with the stones of the field: and the beasts of the field shall be at peace with thee.* **24** *And thou shalt know that thy tabernacle shall be in peace; and thou shalt visit thy habitation, and shalt not sin.* **25** *Thou shalt know also that thy seed shall be great, and thine offspring as the grass of the earth.* **26** *Thou shalt come to thy grave in a full age, like as a shock of corn cometh in in his season.*

Roughly paraphrased, Eliphaz was saying, "If you will just stop being a godless heathen and will start praying and will listen to my advice, your whole life from this point forward will be absolutely groovy, man..."

But it is his closing statement that is really infuriating:

Job 5:27 *Lo this, we have searched it, so it is; hear it, and know thou it for thy good.*

"Job, there is no need for discussion about this; we have checked on whether or not we are right, and we are right. Hear our lofty wisdom, and be blessed."

It is really hard to fight the gag reflex over that, isn't it? Don't you just love people who are absolutely never wrong, and they know they are never wrong because they have checked and they are never wrong?

There is a little-known yet wonderful superpower that all of us would do good to seek after. It is called "humility." It is sort of like X-ray vision, only better. X-ray vision lets a superhero see the flaws and weaknesses in others; humility lets a person see the flaws and weaknesses in himself. It allows us to concede that we may possibly be wrong from time to time and, therefore, makes us much more careful before we speak.

DO be a real superhero; the world could use a few Humblemans and Humblewomans!

Personal Notes:

_____
_____
_____
_____
_____
_____
_____
_____
_____
_____
_____

Devotion 81

Job had character enough to allow Eliphaz to speak uninterrupted until he was done. But he also had gumption enough to speak up against the false accusations he had just endured.

Job 6:1 *But Job answered and said,* **2** *Oh that my grief were throughly weighed, and my calamity laid in the balances together!* **3** *For now it would be heavier than the sand of the sea: therefore my words are swallowed up.*

Throughout Eliphaz's two-chapter opening diatribe, he made it very clear that he thought Job should not be complaining over what was happening to him and his family. In answer, Job utilized the picture of a scale. He desired that, if it were possible, his grief, what he had gone through and what he was saying about it, could be laid on one side of the scale and the calamity he had and was enduring on the other side of the scale. He believed that it, his calamity, would be heavier than the sand of the sea and, therefore, heavier by far than the words he had spoken about it.

His conclusion of that picture was, "Therefore, because of this, my words are swallowed up." That descriptive phrase "swallowed up" in this case means broken and unrefined.

In other words, Eliphaz was speaking eloquently in response to Job's decidedly un-elegant complaining. But Job had no intention of apologizing for not speaking as eloquently as Eliphaz since Eliphaz was not speaking from a shattered heart and a broken body.

If we are not careful, it will be easy for us to hear harsh and even coarse words that people speak and never stop to think that they may be coming from a place of incredibly deep hurt.

DO give people a lot of grace when they speak from hurt; one day, you yourself may need that same grace.

Personal Notes:

_____

_____

_____

_____

_____

_____

_____

_____

_____

_____

_____

_____

_____

_____

_____

_____

_____

_____

_____

_____

Devotion 82

As Job continued to answer Eliphaz, he utilized some common and easy-to-understand illustrations to prove his point.

Job 6:5 *Doth the wild ass bray when he hath grass? or loweth the ox over his fodder?* **6** *Can that which is unsavoury be eaten without salt? or is there any taste in the white of an egg?* **7** *The things that my soul refused to touch are as my sorrowful meat.*

The braying of the ass and the lowing of the ox in the situation that Job described was their "complaining." They simply would not be doing that if they had plenty of food, meaning if things were going well for them. In the illustration of the unsavory food and the white of an egg, Job was pointing out that they could not be easily eaten without salt. In that illustration, the food and the white of the egg was the calamity he had undergone, and the salt was his ability to complain about it!

If you have ever said, "I just need to vent," then you have verbalized the same argument that Job made here.

Job then said, *"The things that my soul refused to touch are as my sorrowful meat."* By that, he meant that the things he had always dreaded now were being set before him every single day, and he had no choice but to live with them.

And the complaining helped him to do so.

Obviously, there is a great risk here. The Bible is pretty clear that God does not like a murmuring, complaining spirit, and God's people are damaged when they hang around people with a constant negative spirit. But it is also abundantly clear that He knows what we are feeling anyway, and we do not need to pretend otherwise. And lastly, it is clear that there is some help and healing that often takes place when someone sits down and says, "Go ahead and spill your guts; my ear is yours."

DO be a listening ear when needed!

Personal Notes:

_____

_____

_____

_____

_____

_____

_____

_____

_____

_____

_____

_____

_____

_____

_____

_____

_____

Devotion 83

When Job first began to utter his complaint in chapter three, he said that he wished he had never been born. But now, as he answers Eliphaz's ill-timed and inaccurate rebuke, he takes it a step further:

Job 6:8 *Oh that I might have my request; and that God would grant me the thing that I long for!* **9** *Even that it would please God to destroy me; that he would let loose his hand, and cut me off!* **10** *Then should I yet have comfort; yea, I would harden myself in sorrow: let him not spare; for I have not concealed the words of the Holy One.* **11** *What is my strength, that I should hope? and what is mine end, that I should prolong my life?*

In chapter three it was, "I wish I had never been born." And now, in chapter six, it is, "I wish God would just let me die right now." And this will be the first of a great many times that he expresses this desire in the book of Job.

His belief, as we see in verse eleven, is that he had no hope of things ever getting better, and, therefore, no reason to keep on living. Now, we know from reading the end of the book that he was wrong. There is always hope, and therefore, one should never give up! But there is something else, both small and huge all at the same time, that we should take note of. Not only did Job want to die, but he had the means to make it happen:

Job 2:8 *And he took him a potsherd to scrape himself withal; and he sat down among the ashes.*

Joe was right then that very moment holding something sharp enough to do the job. And yet he never did. He had enough respect for God and for the sanctity of life not to do what he desperately wanted to do.

No matter how low you get, no matter how dark the darkness seems, DO be as disciplined as Job in this matter. Your life is not yours to take, and there is always, always, ALWAYS hope, even if you cannot see it!

P.S. No matter who you are, please feel free to reach out to me if you ever get this low; I will be glad to be a friend and a listening ear!

Personal Notes:

_____

_____

_____

_____

_____

_____

_____

_____

_____

_____

_____

_____

_____

_____

Devotion 84

As Job continues his answer to Eliphaz, he asks four consecutive questions designed to illustrate his pitiful condition:

Job 6:12 *Is my strength the strength of stones? or is my flesh of brass? 13 Is not my help in me? and is wisdom driven quite from me?*

The questions found in verse twelve are not hard to understand. Job was reminding his attacking friends that he was going through the worst of agony and that he was merely a creature of flesh and bones rather than one of rock and brass. Some mythical demi-god may well be able to endure such agony, but a human being is not so fortunate.

The third question is a bit more subtle. By asking, "*Is not my help in me?*" he was saying, "The only one I have to help me is me, and that is a pitiful help indeed!" And humanly speaking, he was correct. His kids were all dead, his wife was telling him to go ahead and die, and his friends were ripping him to shreds.

His fourth question meant, "I am not crazy; my body is wrecked, but my mind and my judgment are sound."

But, as you may have already surmised, the one thing Job missed was in the third question. Yes, humanly speaking, he was all he had, but "humanity" is not all there is! There was a God in heaven very much aware of all that was happening and Who had already planned to turn the tide in Job's favor.

DO know that even if you are all you have, you are never all you have!

Personal Notes:

_____
_____
_____
_____
_____
_____
_____
_____
_____
_____
_____
_____
_____
_____
_____
_____
_____
_____
_____
_____
_____
_____
_____
_____
_____
_____

Devotion 85

Job has been the target of his friend's attacks, and now he is going to turn the barrel toward them and say some very uncomfortable things that they need to hear.

Job 6:14 *To him that is afflicted pity should be shewed from his friend; but he forsaketh the fear of the Almighty.* **15** *My brethren have dealt deceitfully as a brook, and as the stream of brooks they pass away;* **16** *Which are blackish by reason of the ice, and wherein the snow is hid:* **17** *What time they wax warm, they vanish: when it is hot, they are consumed out of their place.* **18** *The paths of their way are turned aside; they go to nothing, and perish.* **19** *The troops of Tema looked, the companies of Sheba waited for them.* **20** *They were confounded because they had hoped; they came thither, and were ashamed.* **21** *For now ye are nothing; ye see my casting down, and are afraid.*

If it sounds to you sort of like verse fourteen is a direct stab at Eliphaz, let me help you: it is. The "he" in "he forsaketh the fear of the Almighty" was point-blank and openly being directed at Eliphaz. Job was accusing Eliphaz of disrespecting God by attacking his innocent friend, Job. And all three of them were the evil "my brethren" of verse fifteen. They came promising comfort and yet were as deceitful as an iced-over river that one dare not put any weight on.

And why were they like this?

Fear.

Job said in verse twenty-one, "*For now ye are nothing; ye see my casting down, and are afraid.*" They were afraid that if it happened to Job, it could happen to them, and so they were lashing out at him to appease the God whom they viewed as angry and vindictive. Their view of God was almost as flawed as their view of Job, and their miserable theology produced a miserable assistance.

Before you try to deal with anyone about anything, DO hold your arms out beside you as wide as you can and imagine them pierced with nails. And then say, "If God loves them this much, I shall do the same."

Personal Notes:

_____

_____

_____

_____

_____

_____

_____

_____

_____

_____

_____

_____

_____

_____

Devotion 86

As Job continues answering Eliphaz, he deals with something that they had not said, but that he was certain they had in mind.

Job 6:22 *Did I say, Bring unto me? or, Give a reward for me of your substance?* **23** *Or, Deliver me from the enemy's hand? or, Redeem me from the hand of the mighty?*

When someone has encountered a financial disaster or gotten themselves into some kind of huge trouble, what are you expecting when they call you up? Clearly, you are expecting the typical, "Hey, can you help me out with a chunk of cash? Can you pay my bail? Can you fix this?" And obviously, human nature is to bristle at people who cause all of their own problems and then expect others to pay for them.

But not only had Job not done this with his friends, he did not even ask them to come! They had no reason to treat him like a parasite because he was not looking for anything from anyone. And, it is that truth that led Job into his assertion of the next two verses:

Job 6:24 *Teach me, and I will hold my tongue: and cause me to understand wherein I have erred.* **25** *How forcible are right words! but what doth your arguing reprove?*

In other words, his attackers had no proof of what they were saying or of what they were clearly inferring, and yet their words kept coming. Right words, words that are grounded in facts and proof, are indeed forcible, but hurling unfounded arguments accomplishes absolutely nothing.

Before you ever argue with anyone about anything, DO get your facts in order. And if, in that attempt, you find that you do not actually have any facts to get in order, DO shut up!

Personal Notes:

_____

_____

_____

_____

_____

_____

_____

_____

_____

_____

_____

_____

_____

_____

_____

_____

_____

_____

_____

_____

_____

_____

Devotion 87

As chapter six draws to a close, Job, who has been leveling some accurate and devastating accusations against his friends, now makes an appeal to their hearts.

Job 6:26 *Do ye imagine to reprove words, and the speeches of one that is desperate, which are as wind?* **27** *Yea, ye overwhelm the fatherless, and ye dig a pit for your friend.* **28** *Now therefore be content, look upon me; for it is evident unto you if I lie.* **29** *Return, I pray you, let it not be iniquity; yea, return again, my righteousness is in it.* **30** *Is there iniquity in my tongue? cannot my taste discern perverse things?*

In verse twenty-six, Job pointed out that they were ripping him to shreds based only on his words, his desperate speeches. They could not find any flaw in his conduct, so they were castigating him for his complaint. He goes on to tell them that they are overwhelming the fatherless, him, and digging a pit for their own friend. Then he tells them to be content, meaning to please just stop and let it be enough; they should be able to look at him and tell that he is not lying. He is still able to discern right from wrong, and he has done nothing wrong.

Does it strike you in all of this that these men are making one critical mistake? They are trying to play God and do His job! If Job is indeed as wicked as these men say, then God will deal with him. But what is the point in their continued badgering when they have literally no proof whatsoever that Job has done a single thing wrong? If they had any evidence, anything they could point to, the conversation would be worth having. But if not, then why continue hurting someone you claim to love?

DO know the difference between facts and feelings; "I saw you do this" is very different from "Well, I think..."!

Personal Notes:

_____
_____
_____
_____
_____
_____
_____
_____
_____
_____
_____
_____
_____
_____
_____
_____
_____
_____
_____
_____
_____
_____

Devotion 88

As chapter seven begins, Job returns once more to his pitiful plight. And the details he gives are heart-wrenching indeed.

Job 7:1 *Is there not an appointed time to man upon earth? are not his days also like the days of an hireling?* **2** *As a servant earnestly desireth the shadow, and as an hireling looketh for the reward of his work:* **3** *So am I made to possess months of vanity, and wearisome nights are appointed to me.* **4** *When I lie down, I say, When shall I arise, and the night be gone? and I am full of tossings to and fro unto the dawning of the day.* **5** *My flesh is clothed with worms and clods of dust; my skin is broken, and become loathsome.* **6** *My days are swifter than a weaver's shuttle, and are spent without hope.*

Job argued that just like an employee in the field, a hireling, bears the heat of the day and yet looks forward to the cool shadows of the night, he was looking forward to death so that his suffering could come to an end. And verse three begins to put a time element to all of this; it had been going on for months. Before these men ever heard of his tragedy and got their things together and made their way to him, he had already been suffering for months.

How bad was it? When he went to bed each night, it brought him no comfort; he was so miserable that he just wished it was time to go ahead and wake up; he had worms crawling in and on the open sores

180

of his body; his skin was broken open, putrid, and gut-wrenching to smell. Verse six is a phrase that means he was getting old way before his time and had no hope of things getting better.

So much of his complaint dealt with time. But the good news for us, news that he did not yet understand, is that the God who holds time in His hands also holds the ability to change what happens in time. Job thought only of death and rest, but each day that he continued to live he was actually one day closer to deliverance and restoration.

If you are going through the fire and there seems to be no hope, DO use this phrase often: "I don't know how long it will last, but I do know I am one day closer to being through it than I was yesterday!"

Personal Notes:

_____

_____

_____

_____

_____

_____

_____

_____

_____

_____

_____

_____

Devotion 89

Up until this point in the text, Job has been addressing and arguing with his friends. But beginning in verse eight, a unique change takes place.

Job 7:8 *The eye of him that hath seen me shall see me no more: thine eyes are upon me, and I am not.* **9** *As the cloud is consumed and vanisheth away: so he that goeth down to the grave shall come up no more.* **10** *He shall return no more to his house, neither shall his place know him any more.* **11** *Therefore I will not refrain my mouth; I will speak in the anguish of my spirit; I will complain in the bitterness of my soul.* **12** *Am I a sea, or a whale, that thou settest a watch over me?* **13** *When I say, My bed shall comfort me, my couch shall ease my complaint;* **14** *Then thou scarest me with dreams, and terrifiest me through visions:*

Notice the words "thine" in verse eight and "thou" in verses twelve and fourteen. Both the grammar and the details let us know that Job has now stopped talking to and about his "frienemies," and is now talking to God. He views God as one who is intently watching him at every moment, and not for good reasons. In verse twelve, he asks God if He looks at him as if he is as dangerous as the ocean or a whale, and therefore has set barriers up that he cannot pass. And then in verses thirteen and fourteen, he lets us, and his friends, in on another part of his torment.

Job was having nightmares.

This poor man was going through it! How awful would it be for your waking hours to be a living torment, and then to find your sleeping hours filled with nightmares!

Now, there was nothing his three attackers could see that would let them know that. All they could see were ten graves and a body covered in boils. And they based everything they said on what they could see. Maybe, just maybe if they had also known about the nightmares, they would have had a bit more pity.

But isn't it usually like that? We never really know all that a person is going through, now do we? So, since that is the case, just to be safe, DO extend a bit more mercy than you think is warranted, just in case you don't yet know everything that a person is facing!

Personal Notes:

_____
_____
_____
_____
_____
_____
_____
_____
_____
_____
_____
_____

Devotion 90

As Job continues speaking aloud to God in the presence of his three tormentors, he asks a series of seven straight questions.

Job 7:17 *What is man, that thou shouldest magnify him? and that thou shouldest set thine heart upon him?* **18** *And that thou shouldest visit him every morning, and try him every moment?* **19** *How long wilt thou not depart from me, nor let me alone till I swallow down my spittle?* **20** *I have sinned; what shall I do unto thee, O thou preserver of men? why hast thou set me as a mark against thee, so that I am a burden to myself?* **21** *And why dost thou not pardon my transgression, and take away mine iniquity? for now shall I sleep in the dust; and thou shalt seek me in the morning, but I shall not be.*

Taken together, all of those questions are Job's way of asking, "Am I really important enough to warrant this kind of constant attention?" In Job's view, it seemed that the most important thing in God's sight was tormenting Job every single second of every single day. Job clearly once again mistook who it was that was tormenting him; it was Satan, not God.

And yet, in the midst of that error, Job swerved into some truths about God. He spoke of sin in verse twenty, indicating that God is holy. He called God the preserver of men, indicating that God is sovereign. He spelled out that God pardons transgression and takes away iniquity, indicating that God is merciful.

And since we have something that Job did not have, the completed revelation of Scripture, the even better news, from our perspective, is that this is the kind of constant attention God gives us, not what Job thought God was giving him! Every moment of every day our holy God has, as His primary focus, redeeming fallen man!

If you want to know the real heartbeat of God, rather than doing as Job and focusing on your own wounds, DO focus on HIS wounds, freely received for you!

Personal Notes:

_____

_____

_____

_____

_____

_____

_____

_____

_____

_____

_____

_____

_____

_____

_____

_____

_____

Devotion 91

Perhaps the most bitter thing you will ever taste are the words that someone else puts in your mouth. Job was about to experience that, courtesy of his second attacker, Bildad.

Job 8:1 *Then answered Bildad the Shuhite, and said,* **2** *How long wilt thou speak these things? and how long shall the words of thy mouth be like a strong wind?* **3** *Doth God pervert judgment? or doth the Almighty pervert justice?*

If you have ever heard someone described as "being full of hot air," you know what it means when Bildad said, "how long shall the words of thy mouth be like a strong wind?"

But that petty insult pales in comparison to what came next:

Job 8:3 *Doth God pervert judgment? or doth the Almighty pervert justice?*

Those two phrases are nearly identical in meaning, any differences between them are very slight indeed. Bildad was being intentionally repetitive and accusing Job of accusing God this way. And yet, the word "pervert" only occurs three times in the book of Job, and none of them were spoken by Job. In fact, that word did not come out of anyone's mouth until right here when Bildad said it! Just a few seconds earlier, in fact, Job had said the words "I have sinned" (Job 7:20).

In his pain and anguish throughout this account, Job clearly did not get everything right about God. But accusing God of perverting judgment and justice is not one of the things that he got wrong.

DO stop for a moment and think of a time when someone put words in your mouth. Did you like it? Very doubtful. So DO avoid putting words in the mouths of others!

Personal Notes:

_____

_____

_____

_____

_____

_____

_____

_____

_____

_____

_____

_____

_____

_____

_____

_____

_____

_____

_____

_____

Devotion 92

Continuing on in his ill-founded diatribe, Bildad now chose to wield the horrible power of "if."

Job 8:4 *IF thy children have sinned against him, and he have cast them away for their transgression;* **5** *IF thou wouldest seek unto God betimes, and make thy supplication to the Almighty;* **6** *IF thou wert pure and upright; surely now he would awake for thee, and make the habitation of thy righteousness prosperous.*

If. Bildad did not actually say Job's ten children were dead because they had sinned, he merely "iffed" it. He did not actually say that Job was not seeking God and praying, he merely "iffed" it. He did not actually say that Job was so filthy that God had turned away from him and taken a nap so as not to have to look at him, he merely "iffed" it.

If. If. If.

In case you do not know, an "if" used in this manner is the weapon used by someone who is seeking cover as they wield it. It is the tool of the timid, the mace of the mouse-like, and the cudgel of the coward. It is a cheap cologne masquerading as bravery, a theological "Hai-Karate" whose two main ingredients are laziness and self-righteousness.

If "if" is the best you have when trying to "set someone straight," you would be better served quietly signing up for "Learning To Keep Your Mouth Shut, 101."

IF you are in the habit of attacking others with ifs, DO choose to keep all of your ifs to yourself from this moment forward, since you will appreciate them more than anyone else anyway!

Personal Notes:

_____

_____

_____

_____

_____

_____

_____

_____

_____

_____

_____

_____

_____

_____

_____

_____

_____

_____

_____

_____

_____

_____

_____

Devotion 93

At some point, it seems to have occurred to Bildad that he was making a lot of assertions but not offering any proof. Thus, he quickly tried to lay a foundation under the shaky structure he already spent several verses building.

Job 8:8 *For enquire, I pray thee, of the former age, and prepare thyself to the search of their fathers:* **9** *(For we are but of yesterday, and know nothing, because our days upon earth are a shadow:)* **10** *Shall not they teach thee, and tell thee, and utter words out of their heart?*

Verse eight gives us a very interesting phrase to consider, "the former age." It seems clearly to be referring to the age prior to the flood. The internal evidence of the book indicates that Job seems to have lived sometime shortly after the flood. The Septuagint opines that he reached the age of about 270, which would put him just a bit before the time of Abraham.

It is ironic to consider that that long of a lifespan was regarded by Bildad as being merely a shadow. But since people prior to the flood lived eight and nine hundred years, it makes sense from his perspective.

But the main point to be garnered here is that Bildad was pointing back to "the way those old guys back there thought" as proof that he was right in his views. But if the old-timers were always right, why, pray tell, did God have to flood the earth to begin with?

There is a careful balance to be struck here. It is foolish to discard everything that people before us said and thought and believed. But it is equally foolish to cling to everything that people before us said and thought and believed! And while people in Job's day, who did not have a scrap of Scripture to read, may perhaps be excused for basing their beliefs and practices on men of the past, no one in our day, who has the completed canon of Scripture, can now be excused for so doing.

DO respect men of the past, but DO also ground all of your beliefs and practices on the Scripture that you hold in your hands right now in the present!

Personal Notes:

_____

_____

_____

_____

_____

_____

_____

_____

_____

_____

_____

_____

Devotion 94

As Bildad brought his first attack against Job to a close, he used a word someone else already used a few times in this book.

Job 8:20 *Behold, God will not cast away a PERFECT man, neither will he help the evil doers:* **21** *Till he fill thy mouth with laughing, and thy lips with rejoicing.* **22** *They that hate thee shall be clothed with shame; and the dwelling place of the wicked shall come to nought.*

Bildad's argument was that, since Job had clearly been "cast away by God," he could not possibly be perfect. And that word does not mean flawless in every way, it means "innocent, morally pure, and complete."

I assume you remember where you have heard those words in this book before:

Job 1:1 *There was a man in the land of Uz, whose name was Job; and that man was PERFECT and upright, and one that feared God, and eschewed evil.*

Job 1:8 *And the LORD said unto Satan, Hast thou considered my servant Job, that there is none like him in the earth, a PERFECT and an upright man, one that feareth God, and escheweth evil?*

Job 2:3 *And the LORD said unto Satan, Hast thou considered my servant Job, that there is none like him in the earth, a PERFECT and an upright man, one that feareth God, and escheweth evil? and* *still he holdeth fast his integrity, although thou movedst me against him, to destroy him without cause.*

Ahem.

What we have here is a disagreement between Bildad and God. And, to put it in country vernacular, "Imma hafta go with God on this."

DO remember that what others THINK about you (good or bad!) is nowhere near as significant as what God KNOWS about you!

Personal Notes:

_____

_____

_____

_____

_____

_____

_____

_____

_____

_____

_____

_____

_____

_____

_____

_____

_____

_____

_____

_____

Devotionals

DO Drops Volume 1
DO Drops Volume 2
DO Drops Volume 3
DO Drops Volume 4
DO Drops Volume 5
DO Drops Volume 6
DO Drops Volume 7
DO Drops Volume 8
DO Drops Volume 9
DO Drops Volume 10

More Books by Dr. Bo Wagner

Beyond the Colored Coat
Don't Muzzle the Ox
From Footers to Finish Nails
I'm Saved! Now What???
Learning Not to Fear the Old Testament
Marriage Makers/Marriage Breakers
Daniel: Breathtaking
Esther: Five Feast and the Fingerprints of God
Ephesians: Treasures of Family
Galatians: Treasures of Liberty
James: The Pen and the Plumb Line
Jonah: A Study in Greatness
Nehemiah: A Labor of Love
Proverbs: Bright Lights from Dark Sayings Vol 1
Proverbs: Bright Lights from Dark Sayings Vol 2
Romans: Salvation From A-Z
Ruth: Diamonds in the Darkness
The Revelation: Ready or Not

Books in the Night Heroes Series

Cry From the Coal Mine (Vol. 1)
Free Fall (Vol. 2)
Broken Brotherhood (Vol. 3)
The Blade of Black Crow (Vol. 4)
Ghost Ship (Vol. 5)
When Serpents Rise (Vol. 6)
Moth Man (Vol. 7)
Runaway (Vol. 8)
Terror by Day (Vol. 9)
Winter Wolf (Vol. 10)
Desert Heat (Vol. 11)

Sci-Fi

Zak Blue and the Great Space Chase Series:
Falcon Wing (Vol. 1)
Enter the Maelstrom (Vol. 2)